CHASING IMPACT

RYAN LUCHAU

WESTBOW
PRESS®
A DIVISION OF THOMAS NELSON
& ZONDERVAN

WestBow Press books may be ordered through booksellers or by contacting:

WestBow Press
A Division of Thomas Nelson & Zondervan
1663 Liberty Drive
Bloomington, IN 47403
www.westbowpress.com
844-714-3454

ISBN: 978-1-6642-3189-4 (sc)
ISBN: 978-1-6642-3190-0 (hc)
ISBN: 978-1-6642-3188-7 (e)

Library of Congress Control Number: 2021908218

Print information available on the last page.

WestBow Press rev. date: 05/11/2021

To my wife, Angie, and our kids, Gabbi, Caden, Silas, and baby Emme, who is a new part of our story. You mean the world to me, and I thank God daily that I am a part of your journey.

> For the sun rises with its scorching heat and withers the grass; its flower falls, and its beauty perishes. So also, will the rich man fade away in the midst of his pursuits.
> —James 1:9–11

CONTENTS

INTRODUCTION

This book has been on my heart to write now for a while, and now seems to be as good a time as any to put these thoughts and experiences on paper and share. It may not be clear why you found this book, but I trust that you will be able to glean something from it by identifying the opportunity to make a little bigger dent in the world and placing energy behind your "just cause" that gets you up in the morning, essentially living in soul purpose, or impact.

I am not a professional athlete or actor. I haven't written any books before and surely don't have the accolades to be recognized as anyone significant. I am just an unapologetical Christian and small-town Montana kid at heart with a desire to make an impact. Impact—some are chasing it, others are living in it, and frankly many will never grasp the significance of it.

I might say that this is my attempt to share my heart and story and how I have been able to grow as a Christian man, fail miserably, and recognize the significance of being able to pursue making an impact—one step (not always forward)—at a time. The book will also share what has proven to be useful in helping others thrive through a faith-based lens.

What I am going to share in practical guidance is not anything complicated; it includes very basic and fundamental Christian principles that, when focused on, helps us develop resiliency and resolve to face the challenges of everyday life.

We all have a story to tell, and that is what builds in us the unique perception in which we see the world. While my values have certainly been built around my personal story, environment, and people who have influenced me, my faith in God and Jesus as my Savior is the lens through which these values and this belief system are lived out. This has not always been the case, but since embarking on this journey of faith, the trajectory of my life and how I perceive and navigate through challenges that come with it have changed exponentially.

Some of my story that seems pertinent to share includes growing up in Montana and living here for all but approximately five years. It is not the time in Montana but instead the time I have spent outside my great state that is relevant.

My first adventure outside Montana was going to college in Las Vegas. I would genuinely correlate my college experience to my first character-building opportunity, as it was completely out of the realm of expectations for me to leave the state for school, and likely because of this, I decided to venture away from home.

The problem with this is that because a foundation of character, morals, and discipline had not been established (parents, take note) my experience in Vegas resulted in more time as an eighteen-year-old in the sports books and casinos than it actually did in the classroom. It bears noting that the legal gambling age in Nevada was and is still twenty-one years of age. I wish I could say it was, but I can humbly admit this was not my first or last true bout with addiction. It wasn't until after a life-altering loss of a close childhood friend that I determined that it was best for me to get back to Montana to be closer to friends and family. Unfortunately the story of addiction did not end there, but despite being away from Las Vegas and the incredible temptation of gambling and alcohol, the pursuit for pleasure did not go away.

Leading up to my late twenties, I had struggled with bouts of alcoholism, pornography, material gain through debt, and toxic relationships. And it took me a while to realize the path I was heading down was simply going to lead me down a path to self-destruction.

I was chasing something in my life, like many of us do, but I was chasing pleasure. I was chasing the exact same thing that I had come to connect with subconsciously; the more I chased pleasure, the emptier I felt. That was beginning to be my story, emptiness and despair.

In this story of trials and tribulations, you will also find a story of redemption. After my first deployment to Iraq in 2004 and coming home, hearing in Kuwait about the challenges we would face, I chuckled in my heart at an individual giving a brief about what to expect when we returned and the challenges we would likely face.

I laughed simply because I had (vainly) realized that I would be living my dream life because I was a young, single man in the best physical condition of my life and had no debt and a little bit of money for the first time in my life.

My dream life included finding my dream woman, enjoying what I recognized at the time as a trendy social life, traveling, and playing excessive amounts of golf (not necessarily in that order). Those really were the only things I was concerned with. Everything else in my life would fit around these pleasure-filled conveniences. It was just into my second month home that my life would take a turn toward redemption.

In May 2005 at a gathering that was supposed to consist of just a few guy friends, I was introduced to a woman who was brought into my life to help save me from myself. The only explanation for this chance occurrence is God's handiwork and a lot of prayer from those closest to me, especially my mother. Fourteen years and four children later—ironically, doctors told us early on in our marriage that my wife would not be successful in having children—we are journeying through our midlife trusting the plan and course that has been laid out for us.

Now having been back from my second deployment since March 2019, I find myself chasing something probably more than I have ever pursued anything in life, but in this case, it is a positive pursuit.

Whether we are chasing or living in impact, it will be at a cost to something else. We will be compromising something in our lives. My intent for writing this book is to help determine what that compromise is, to help the reader understand the importance of it, and to bring light to the significance of the compromise. I especially want to articulate why our Christian faith cannot be part of that compromise. Our relationship with Jesus, who gave it all for us, has to be lived out reciprocally. Living it out is through our expression in everything we do as a sign of our belief in God's inspired and holy Word, our complete trust in Jesus as the Son of God and Savior of our sins, and our obedience to his will for our lives, all so God can get the glory for what he has done.

Impact, as I will demonstrate, is not about us but instead about God receiving glory from our lives, which without faith and in a secular context we would be seeking the recognition, or the glory, for. Through the Christian lens, the glory and recognition shed off us and point toward Jesus because our lives are no longer ours. Instead we are to live for Jesus.

CHAPTER 1

IMPACT IS ...

JUST A FEW SHORT WEEKS prior to starting this project, as I was attending a volunteer dinner hosted by our church, I listened to the guest speaker discuss his role in a national faith-based nonprofit and how he recognized a need to take a step back from his role as executive director and be content with not being in the limelight for a while. This truly resonated with me and made me reflect on some of the big pursuits and responsibilities in my life.

What also really resonated with me during that dinner was the question posed by the guest speaker, "If your life were represented by a book title, what would the name of the book be?"

How perfect of an opportunity for me to reflect on the title for the book that I was about to embark on. So as I considered this that night and all of the things currently active in my life, I could not help but think that the title of my first book would be *Chasing Impact*, a title I had selected long before the first words were written.

Chasing Impact means something a little different at this point in my life than it would have fifteen years ago. Part of my personal challenge navigating life as a young Christian came through not being concerned with reconciling faith with my physical health, social life, or other areas of wellness. My desire to continue hanging out with the friends I grew up with did not coincide with my faith journey. And my financial brokenness was not going to work as I attempted to align faith with all-things wellness. My faith was all about me and did not indicate a changed heart.

Out of the process of reconciling, doing things as they align with scripture, came a revelation. The revelation was later validated in my work as a chaplain.

Throughout my time as a chaplain, the vast majority of my conversations with soldiers outside the Christian faith revolved around issues that had to do with six areas. The counseling for these soldiers was centered on navigating their challenges through a lens that would help them establish new, healthy disciplines. And out of this came what I now refer to as the *thrive factors*.

Once I recognized this, it was easier to work with the soldiers and their families. These six areas all tend to take dominion over one's life, so my guidance was an attempt to help the soldiers traverse through potentially challenging areas and get them to a point where the challenges were energy-producing, not depleting. All the while, I built relationships and trust with them so we could have genuine conversations—in many cases, eventually leading to conversations about genuine faith.

Interestingly these thrive factors were part of our original support model for Impact Montana. They were just called wellness pillars. Impact Montana is an organization that was established in 2014 to support service members, veterans, and their families in Montana. Regardless of what they are called, they have all been an incredibly important part of my faith-based journey.

In case you are wondering what these thrive factors are, I will share them briefly here and expand on their relevance in a subsequent section. These factors are spiritual health and wellness, physical health and wellness, social wellness, family wellness, financial wellness, and career wellness.

I listed spiritual health and wellness first because this particular factor builds the perspective and the lens through which all others are optimally viewed. Again, we will dissect these factors later, but understanding what they are early on will help correlate impact with thriving.

Anyone can assume what "impact" means based on the correlation to thriving, and naturally when someone is chasing something, that person has not been able to achieve what they are pursuing. I will attempt to articulate how much of our ability to thrive and be impactful is derived from the lens through which we perceive the world.

I have worked with people from all walks of life, including homeless veterans, and I have realized that some of the spiritually richest individuals have no material possessions and very little money but thrive in their own way because they have a profound faith in and love for Jesus Christ and recognition of their soul's purpose. How we thrive is unique to each and every one of us, but it is directly related to a connection with God.

On the contrary, some of the richest, most materially wealthy, or most intellectually savvy individuals I have known are broken and without hope, and their actions and attitudes toward others reflect that.

So thriving, or impact, has no direct correlation with material wealth but instead is correlated with hope, a connection to others, living with purpose, and an identity found in faith, not in wealth, career, marital status, or what one drives.

Whether one finds doom and gloom or sees opportunities through struggles, observes value in facing adversity, and has character growth through suffering are all relative to their perspective. (See Romans 5 for the apostle Paul's perspective on this.)

To continue on this journey, it is necessary to give the baseline for what we are considering. *Merriam Webster's Dictionary* defines "impact" as "having a direct effect or impact on" or "to impinge or make contact especially forcefully," which I would say leaves the definition of the word significantly short of its potential. So we are going to expand the definition of "impact" a bit by looking at it through a Christian lens.

Impact, for our sake, will be defined as the connection to one's soul's purpose relative to their ability to enhance others' lives by living out biblical faith. Impact is clearly one's soul's mission and a contributing factor to building a legacy. "Chasing impact" means never giving up a pursuit of the purpose that has been set before you; it is the relentless pursuit of God's vision or tug on the heart for a specific mission, all the while giving God the glory.

It is all about our faith in action, specifically to give God his due glory. Simply stated, "impact" is not just about making a difference, being goal-oriented, or having dreams or a successful career. Impact is the pursuit of a vision and the impression of a legacy, neither of which, in a biblical context, has anything to do with ourselves.

The beauty of the type of impact I am speaking of is that it is not strictly a science; nor is it strictly an art. Instead it is a combination of both science and art through the lens of faith. Impact is measured in God's economic terms, not ours. Just like art, it also looks different to and is judged independently by everyone and certainly is relative to the lens through which it is being perceived.

The argument I will make in this book is that one's impact correlates with faith and aligns with one's particular purpose. The "one" may in fact be an individual or family, community, or organization. We will hone in on the impact generated by an individual and how that affects family, those around the individual, and the community, and we will save organizational impact for another day.

Before moving on, I would like to clarify that our soul's purpose is not about us but about what we can do to influence the world for Jesus. On the other hand, we have to recognize that there is a type of purpose that makes us feel good yet is not necessarily about anything other than us. We must establish the difference to better understand the kind of impact being discussed relative to purpose.

When I think of the term "chasing impact," I think of the active involvement of pursuing something but never being able to reach it. This could bring a negative connotation to the term; however, I will say that chasing impact is not negative because if you are pursuing impact, as we are discussing it, that just means there is a noble intent to do good and make a difference in the world in Jesus's name.

When someone is chasing impact or living an influential life, that person is on the right track, making a difference for others, and living out the gospel and the Great Commission (Matthew 28:19). This is the kind of energy that I hope to generate with this work, being able to recognize that making an impact is about others, transcending our own capabilities, and finding a pursuit that outlives us. In essence, impact is not really about whether someone is chasing it or living in it; the point is the target, or proximal connection to God as the motivation.

Christian, God has ordained you for a specific soul purpose. You just may not completely recognize the significance of that purpose yet. It is perhaps because you have nested in the comfort of God's grace and have to get out of the comfort of that nest in order to chase the impact that God is calling you to. Getting out of that nest will mean broadening your perspective and honing in on beginning to see the world through the lens God has shared with us through his holy Word. It is my prayer that this book will be a blessing and additional encouragement to help you find out what God is calling you to that will allow you to honor him.

Let me be clear in saying that your ultimate source for clarity, identifying soul purpose for building your relationship with God, is through the Bible. No book can and will ever replace the need to get in God's Word and intimately know him as he desires a relationship with you. The purest way to gain the perspective you need for impact is to get to know and communicate with God through the Bible. He is the source for your impact.

CHAPTER 2

UNDERSTANDING THE VITALITY OF PERSPECTIVE

SATISFACTION DOES NOT COME FROM letting the status quo remain and extraordinary dormant. Satisfaction comes from knowing that when the status quo is not good enough, that an extraordinary effort produces extraordinary results. Purposeful passion and pursuit of the extraordinary produces dynamic results. Most importantly, do not let internal or external fear prevent you from pursuing and producing soul-purpose and passion. Are you satisfied with the status quo?

The previous thought is from August 2016 in the midst of waiting on a Chaplain Accession's Board determination and whether or not I would end up being approved to serve as a chaplain in the Army National Guard. Interestingly in this particular time frame, I was spinning my wheels in the middle of chasing impact after having been denied confirmation after a May 2016 Chaplain Accessioning Board. My concept of impact at that time was based on identity and whether or not I was going to get the opportunity to serve as a chaplain. This was a case of my flesh getting the best of me and thinking my purpose was connected to serving as a chaplain instead of just being obedient to a call.

Identity has a tremendous influence on our spiritual maturity, and in the midst of this "identity crisis," I recognized that it did not matter if the call to the chaplaincy was going to be fulfilled. What did matter was that I continued to live according to the purpose and meaning God had placed on my life, regardless of there being a cross on my army uniform or not.

Some people get intimidated by failure, and at one point in my life, this was the case for me; however, I have come to appreciate failure because I trust that something of value will come out of it. I also trust that God is allowing me to fail so I can eventually taste the victory of something sweeter, something that God will be given the glory for.

> *Gold Nugget: We can be bogged down by who we think we are, who others say we are, or remaining status quo, or we can be lifted up by who God says we are and the reality of who he is.*

For a time, despite my faith, I was bogged down by who I thought I was after having been denied the initial opportunity to serve as a chaplain.

At other times, I have correlated my identity with my occupation, like when I was adamant about pursuing active-duty chaplaincy after my recent deployment or returning to work to my nonmilitary occupation, getting caught up in the fact that I was not still serving as a chaplain on active duty. Perspective is a significant component to impact, along with the pursuit of it. A transition takes place in our lives when we go from thinking we are the center of attention, to life not being about us.

The moment we realize life is not about us, which is very difficult to accept, but instead about Jesus and others is a pivotal point, which is theologically known as justification. It is also the point when we appreciate that all people have the need to be loved and are loved by God (John 14:6), and because we are made in the image of God, we have a need to be reconciled back to God. This is the moment that we go from sulking in our own miseries or challenges to figuring out, despite our circumstances, that we have a soul purpose and that we can help someone else navigate through their own miseries or challenges by leading them to the gospel and the life-changing ministry of Jesus.

Without this transition in how we see the world and our role in it, we continue to navigate through life with barriers that impede our personal impact. Barriers like competition, ego, and emotional instability, just to name a few, get in the way of our ability to thrive as an individual pursuing something greater than ourselves.

This is easy to see and often found in our hyper-competitive society as it creates barriers to thriving and impact when measurements are on instrumental motivation instead of the intrinsic value of building something collectively.

A competitive and communal spirit are mutually exclusive and impossible to hold in our heart at the exact same time. There is a conflict of interest in our heart if we are attempting to be better than our neighbor, as opposed to working with our neighbor in order to have an optimal living environment through mutual understanding.

Our perspective of community and the value it holds is essential in leveraging others' talents, skills, abilities, and value in contrast to us thinking we have to compete against others' talents, skills, abilities, and values.

What I am attempting to articulate is that perspective as it relates to impact is drawn away from our natural tendencies and ways through which we want to see the world, to a broader scope, or the lens that God sees the world through. This comparison is relative in the context of impact in that if motives are based on personal pursuit, our impact is finite, meaning our impact will not exceed our personal motives.

> *Gold Nugget: If our motives are charged by our relationship with God, a calling placed on our heart, the measure of impact is infinite and something we will never see because it is bigger than us and will outlast our lifetime.*

Further, our values, mindset, goals, and performance reflect our perspective and worldview and serve as temporal or eternal motives. If we are only thinking about leaving our mark on the world, again our impact is finite. But when we are following what we know to be God's calling for our lives, there is eternal, or infinite, value. Perception (eyes on Jesus) is the cornerstone upon which impact is built. Our cornerstone has to be properly set; otherwise our impact is limited (Ephesians 2).

As we see from this experience in pursuing the chaplaincy, perspective was more important than mindset due to the notion that without an understanding of purpose or calling that God had called me toward and was equipping me for, my mindset would have been falsely developed.

I wholeheartedly argue that perspective will influence mindset 100 percent of the time because it is more constant, when the mindset is fluid or presumably in constant change without that cornerstone in which it is set.

I could have easily woken up every day thinking positive thoughts, "hunting the good stuff," or utilizing any other positive psychology approach that floods our culture, but without the cornerstone of my faith in Christ, or perspective, and a source from which to glean mindfulness, it would have been difficult to remain resilient.

Despite our circumstances or the hardships we are facing, we get to influence our mindset and how we are going to respond in a situation based upon our perspective and worldview. Perspective is such a powerful component of our wellness and how we live day to day.

I would boldly state that perspective and keeping our

eyes fixed on Jesus through spiritual disciplines has the most powerful influence on how we approach our marriage and family responsibilities, treat ourselves and others, find success in school or work, we spend our money, attain our overall health and wellness, and influences our mindset.

Worldview/perspective is derived from education, environment, and experience. It is the lens through which we perceive the world and ultimately the source for all things related to spiritual health and wellness. Although it can change over time, it is the innermost conviction of how all facets of our lives are lived. Our spiritual health and resilience start here.

Before we continue, I want to point out the fact our spiritual health and wellness are not solely, nor "soul-ly," dependent on us. Instead it is in direct relationship to what has been, is being, and will be done for us. God has articulated detail after detail of his finely crafted creation through his Word, so we have the blueprint to help us develop the worldview; the rest of the development occurs through the ongoing handiwork of the Holy Spirit, through both the environment we are exposed to and the experiences we encounter. Without the Christian education, we are less inclined to recognize God's handiwork around us and in our lives.

Take, for example, my perception of God prior to committing my life to following Jesus. I was baptized as a baby in a Lutheran church and grew up going to different churches leading to a general understanding of who Jesus was through a multidenominational lens.

As a preteen, I went to an Assembly of God church camp after my parents' divorce, and I can recall one of the camp leaders attempting to get me to speak in tongues. It was very uncomfortable for me, and it really limited my pursuit of anything faith-based for many years. But this is what I knew Christianity to be, not what the Bible or God said it was.

Little did I realize that despite my pursuit ending, I was still being pursued. It was just a matter of time and being introduced to influential events and people that would lead me to turn my life over to Christ.

EDUCATION

While I will leave the topic of our current education system in the United States for another day, it does not discount the role it plays in developing worldview and one's perspective.

More importantly in this conversation is the role of the church as it relates to perspective development. Someone who grows up in a Catholic church is going to hear a vastly different message than someone who grows up in an LDS or Evangelical church. The tenets of faith in each of these faith-based communities drives an individual's perception of God, Jesus, and the Holy Spirit.

What is true—and also unfortunate—is that the leaders of churches and denominations can have more influence in developing one's perspective than the Bible does. At the end of the day, we have to remember that we are called to be faithful followers of Jesus, not faithful followers of man, regardless of their role in leading a church. This is why conforming to a Bible-centric church is much more spiritually rewarding than conforming to a church that values conforming to a denomination or even culture over the Bible.

Education, as it relates to developing a Christian worldview and perspective, is first directly influenced by the Bible and then instruction from seasoned Christians, which may include pastors, lay leaders, trained teachers, or those mature in the Christian faith.

In our culture today, the tendency is to put our faith in a box and live a life trying to fit that box into the convenience of living in the world. It is impossible to align life with worldly pursuits and have faith that is consistent with what Jesus asked of his disciples and frankly what constitutes being a Christian. James 4 highlights this mutual exclusion, which means the more one is pursuing worldly living, the harder it is to align themselves with godly impact.

What we should be doing as Christ followers is to live through a faith-based lens and adapt the world around us to this perspective, which is in large part faith in action, or what *Chasing Impact* is all about. This means our faith should have more influence in our lives than the world. Shrinking our worldly influence increases our faith; better yet, as our faith and relationship with Jesus grows, the influence the world has on us shrinks.

Education in this sense is paramount and the core component to developing perspective, and the earlier one can be biblically instructed, whether through Sunday school or private Christian or home school, the easier it is to separate the disparate lenses. The longer someone has been exposed to worldly influences, the harder it is to initially recognize the spiritual vitality and life that living in Christ offers.

My early experiences as a converted adult Christian eventually led me to pursue a master's degree in divinity after receiving a bachelor of arts in social sciences from a secular institution. This was somewhat difficult because of the stronghold that the world had on me, but I recognized the call leading to the master's degree was God's pursuit of me regardless of my hesitancy.

Because of being inundated in worldly influences, to include a secular education up to a post-secondary level and a military culture, it was more difficult presumably to completely submit my life to Jesus than if I would have had a stronger biblical foundation growing up.

ENVIRONMENT

When it comes to shaping a worldview, our environment plays a direct role, especially because we are going to correlate how we live relative to the environment in which we live. If we have a Christian education to influence how we live, the environment we live in will have less influence over our worldview.

Consider someone who was raised in a home where there were framed pictures of Jesus on the wall or pictures of Bible verses or a man on his knees praying, yet church attendance was sporadic, and there was physical, spousal, and child abuse.

If all the child had as a reflection of who God is by means of parental behavior, we have a dichotomy of what faith looks like. We have a situation where the child's perspective of who God is as our heavenly Father being skewed, with no biblical understanding of our Father's love. The child may have issues reconciling God as a loving Heavenly Father based on their earthly father's influence.

The beauty of God, specifically through the work of the Holy Spirit, is that we are constantly pursued despite our past, despite our education and despite our understanding of scripture. God does not give up on us, his pursuit is relentless, and impact is perfect when we allow him to stop chasing us because of the innate desire in our heart to follow him. His steadfast pursuit indicates how much he in fact loves us.

Even though every person is born loved as part of God's promise found in John 14:6, what is not equitable is our ability to receive love. We could deem this the "love receipt factor," with the factor being the understanding and importance of God being our primary source for love. When one is not under this guise, there is a disconnect in the magnificence of love as a conditioner to help us thrive. Our probability to thrive is higher when we have the proper understanding of love and its highest source. Loving others in a fraction of the way God loves us is an impact generator.

> *Gold Nugget: Love is an equitable conditioner in that when understood biblically, it will allow an ordinary person the ability to thrive spiritually, and when misrepresented or misunderstood, an extraordinary person to live a less than desirable life.*

When we don't have the biblical understanding of God's love for us, we place the value of love on a cultural scale, and its relativity becomes based on one's environment and experiences. The apostle

Paul states the significance of love in his letter to the Church at Corinth (1 Corinthians 13:13), when he implies out of faith, hope, and love, love holds the greatest value. And the ultimate act of love is demonstrated by the death of Jesus Christ on the cross for you and me.

EXPERIENCES

The third component that helps construct worldview and perspective is experience. While environment is inclusive of the culture one finds themselves in over a period, experiences are an event captured at any point in time that is indicative of an intervening spiritual force, which could in fact be good or evil. An unexplainable survival from a disastrous car wreck, a "chance" reintroduction to someone after years of separation, survival from a botched abortion, or recovery from addiction when all other interventions failed are all events that those looking at life through a Christian lens can explain as miracles, and without the lens of Christ, they are simply random occurrences and difficult to even recognize as significant.

Not ironically, as I spent more time in the Bible and surrounding myself with people of faith, I was witness to events and opportunities in my life that would lead me down a completely different path than what I was going down prior to discovering who Jesus actually was.

I found myself in opportunities that were hard to understand why they were happening the way they were. Looking back, it all makes sense because each opportunity led to more growth that would increase the connectivity to impact. Some of these opportunities came from perceived failure, and others came from simply gaining time in spiritual gifts that I did not realize were present.

A Christian worldview is such a powerful tool in that it serves as a lens for life. It is a generator for values. It holds eternal value, offers a macrolevel purview, and is a significant contributor to the capacity of impact.

The Bible, not culture, gives us the basis to define faith, hope, and love and a construct for morality and the discernment to recognize value in failure and the "why" in not having a spirit of fear.

A focus on spiritual health and wellness through the sacrifice of Jesus reshapes challenges associated with mental health into survival through spiritual strength and promotes collaboration and selfless service over competition and selfishness. It gives a person more control because it helps one recognize they have minimal control over things outside themselves. And it promotes the notion that our identity is not found in what we have done but instead by what Christ has done for us. It takes the ego out of our sinful nature and gives all the glory to God.

Essentially a Christian worldview and perspective is the catalyst that propels faith into impact, and without the foundation of faith, we can find ourselves in a quagmire of worldly influences that will drive poor overall health.

CHAPTER 3

A DERIVATIVE OF SPIRITUAL HEALTH

Let love be genuine. Abhor what is evil; hold fast to what is good. Love one another with brotherly affection. Outdo one another in showing honor. Do not be slothful in zeal, be fervent in spirit, serve the Lord. Rejoice in hope, be patient in tribulation, be constant in prayer. Contribute to the needs of the saints and seek to show hospitality. Bless those who persecute you; bless and do not curse them. Rejoice with those who rejoice, weep with those who weep. Live in harmony with one another. Do not be haughty but associate with the lowly. Never be wise in your own sight. Repay no one evil for evil but give thought to do what is honorable in the sight of all. If possible, so far as it depends on you, live peaceably with all. Beloved, never avenge yourselves, but leave it to the wrath of God, for it is written, "Vengeance is mine, I will repay, says the Lord." To the contrary, "if your enemy is hungry, feed him; if he is thirsty, give him something to drink; for by so doing, you will heap burning coals on his head." Do not be overcome by evil, but overcome evil with good.

—Romans 12:9–21

WHEN I THINK OF IMPACT, I think specifically of its relationship with spiritual health. As a former military chaplain, this topic is near and dear to my heart, and because I was not a full-time chaplain for the military, I have had the distinct pleasure of being able to apply this passion to a broader scope than the military. I get to use it in my job working with homeless veterans. I get to use it for nonprofit work, my family, and a pursuit toward entrepreneurship, or, as it is referred to in the veteran's space, Vetrepreneurship.

I strongly believe that our spiritual health is the most important factor in our ability to thrive. Spiritual health has the ability to greatly influence individuals, families, organizations, communities, and nations.

We have taken a look at perspective, which as I argued is the cornerstone for impact, and because impact is a derivative of spiritual health, it serves also as the cornerstone for our spiritual health. How we perceive the world through an understanding of intelligent design, meaning and purpose, morality, our connection to self and others, and hope for the future dictates our ability to be influential. Our spiritual health is based on our understanding of and connection to these things. It is constant and not fluid, as God is constant and unchanging.

Our spiritual health determines our ability to navigate through crises in life. If we do not have an understanding of meaning and purpose, connection to ourselves and others, and hope for the future, our capacity to survive through a crisis is minimal, let alone leaving us any ability to thrive.

Often a taboo subject, spiritual health and wellness is a facet that gets overlooked or significantly discounted when it comes to holistic health. We have already discussed perception to a degree, or the perspective of how one sees the world, which serves as a perfect segue to elaborating on spiritual health.

In my estimation, spiritual health has been discounted because it does not offer the ability to gain quantitative data and scientific measurements like other aspects of comprehensive health and wellness. Gauging the proximal connection one has with life or the world is almost impossible and remains subjective to the point that many of the experts I have worked with don't give it the credence it deserves when it comes to assessing one's functionality in life. My intent here is not to discount the experts' opinions relative to one's ability to function in general, but instead to make the argument that spiritual health is paramount in one's ability to live in impact, or, as we have equated impact to, one's ability to thrive.

As I have experienced in my professional career, spiritual health, as it relates to our conversation and one's ability to thrive personally and professionally or be influential, is a derivative of several key components: faith, hope, love, identity, purpose, connection to community, and morality. This is not to say, however, that spiritual health is only composed of these components, which just happen to be strong conditioners to thriving and ultimately the ability to be impactful.

FAITH

Two main points are pertinent to the discussion on faith as it relates to our intent in articulating impact.

First, faith is not something that can be looked at through a denominational lens, because of interpretations and the placing of our own limits on faith. The temptation with interpretation is to put limitations on faith based on what we interpretively pull from scripture. Along with sharing parables and the profession Jesus made regarding salvation and what he has done for us, we can discern that there is minimal margin for interpretation when it comes to faith. Jesus simply said, "I am the way, and the truth, and the life. No one comes to the Father except through me" (John 14:6). Our imperfections warrant remediation in order to be reunited with a perfect God, and Jesus is that remediation.

Jesus was clear in his ministry by giving a definitive offer, leaving it up to us to consider and receive. If you want the grace and the love, the instructions are easy. Follow him. Because that's the way one receives grace and love and lives in it. Trust Jesus with everything, including the eternal state of your soul. Your eternal security, or salvation, is the free gift of grace. It cannot be earned.

Saving faith is not a matter of simply believing God exists. Saving faith comes by having a posture of total dependence on and complete trust in God. That type of posture is the means by which salvation is received and lives are changed with a perspective shift.

James 2:24 says, "A person is justified by what he does and not by faith alone." What is at stake is the nature of faith that matters to God, not defined by man, as the kind of faith that actually changes lives. Real faith affects what we do by changing our actions. Real faith affects impact.

When James says "faith without works is dead" (James 2:20), he is not saying you need to add a certain level of behavioral compliance in order to be saved. What he means is this: If you claim to believe something but your actions speak otherwise, then you don't actually believe what you think you believe. Your actions are a more reliable indicator than your words. In essence, we may have ulterior motives for influencing others; thus we need to assess our faith and heart through actions.

The second aspect of faith that it is about trusting the object of the faith, not the quality of the faith. Abraham is a great example of this. He is presented frequently in the New Testament as the model for faith from the Old Testament. But if you read and understand his story, you know his faith is presented as a sort of dichotomy.

On one hand, Abraham's canvas was blank. His father was a pagan, which meant Abraham was raised in a pagan world. So his first interaction with a living, omnipotent, intimate God was when God told Abraham to "go from your country and your kindred and your father's house to the land that I will show you. And I will make of you a great nation, and I will bless you and make your name great, so that you will be a blessing. I will bless those who bless you, and him who dishonors you I will curse, and in you all the families of the earth shall be blessed" (Genesis 12:1–3).

And all through Abraham's journey, his faith continued to be tested. He was tested when God told him that he and his wife, Sarah, would have a son (Genesis 20) and when God told him to place his son on the altar for sacrifice (Genesis 22:1–19). And although his faith wavered when he questioned and laughed at God, he, as a spiritually confused man, followed suit, trusting that God would do as he said.

Abraham's story is not a story about Abraham but is instead a story about the might of God. It was better for Abraham to put little faith in a big God than big faith in a little god. This is good news. This is why Jesus says you only need faith the size of a mustard seed. Why? Because it is not about the size of your faith; it's about the size of your God.

It is not the quality of your faith that saves you; it's the object of your faith that saves you and that presents an opportunity for impact. That's the good news of the gospel. That's why Paul inserts this description of God in Romans 4:17, "'He [Abraham] is our father of many nations',—in the presence of the God in whom he believed." What God is that? "The God who gives life to the dead and calls into existence the things that do not exist."

We tend to gauge our faith based on us, not the object. We can't worry about whether we have enough faith. We shouldn't focus on the quality of our faith; instead we should focus on the object of our faith, Jesus as the Son of Abraham's God.

Know that Jesus has changed hearts of stone into hearts of flesh. This knowledge needs to influence the way we live. We can't live our lives based on the quality of our faith. We have to live in the knowledge of who God is. That is saving faith and a worldview worth investing in.

At this point in the book, it warrants a quick pause and opportunity to speak directly to you as the reader, whether you are a mom or dad just trying to catch a breath from the "hectivity" (my personally coined term for chaos) of life, an eighteen-year-old about to graduate and embark on the journey and reality that is life, a transitioning service member who has really had no life outside the military but incredible real-world experience, or an organizational leader who is so consumed with work and career that you feel your priorities may be out of alignment.

We can get wrapped up in the stage of life we are in because it is difficult to slow down enough to control the complexity or stress of each season. But in reality, when we do slow down, we can control our emotions and/or the stress associated with them. Plainly stated, we can either influence the situations we find ourselves in or be consumed by them. And based on what we see in our society overall, many of us are in fact being consumed.

Slowing down and promoting self-awareness occurs when one has a distinct faith, identity, and purpose. When we have a profound investment in these components of spiritual health, the propensity to influence our environment and not be controlled by it is incredibly greater than when we do not have these attributes of spiritual health.

Because we are naturally emotional beings and emotions are physiologically induced, if we are not spiritually conditioned through self-awareness, self-regulation, optimism, mental agility, the ability to live in our character strengths, and a connection to something greater than ourselves (list of Army Master Resilience Training Program Core Competencies), the emotions will run their course and impede our functionality.

Case in point, as a military chaplain who has been introduced to individuals going through perceived personal crises oftentimes leading to suicidal thoughts, it has always been my intent to gauge their spiritual health or let them self-identify their values, their degree of faith, and how they perceive themselves as well as their purpose. The challenge comes when these things are void in their lives, as often one that carries these attributes has the ability to slow down and recognize the value that comes from a life crisis.

One's ability to bounce back from adversity is in its truest form the definition of resilience. Resilience is largely correlated with self-awareness, an ability to regulate in times of stress, and a strong sense of optimism despite the circumstances. So determining the resilience of an individual serves well in determining their risk to self-harm.

Faith is the light that you know is there when you are in complete darkness and having the confidence and endurance to trust that the light will turn on when it is supposed to (John 8:12). It is knowing things are going to be OK even though they are not currently going well.

Having unshakable faith, especially in such a time as this, is hard, but it is not more difficult than any other time in history. We simply just are not generally strong enough in our faith to navigate through turbulent waters because we don't have the comprehension of what faith looks like which will allow us to survive. And we struggle to give up control when it is clear we need to let go.

IDENTITY

"But our citizenship is in heaven, and from it we await a Savior, the Lord Jesus Christ" (Philippians 3:20).

Just like faith, identity is an integral part of our spiritual health. The world says we are defined by our status in society, which has created this false notion that unless we have a certain status or have achieved certain things, we don't really amount to much. According to the world, our status hangs in the balance of where we went to college, career success, our political persuasion, how much money we make, or, if we are talking military terms, our rank.

This is dangerous because of its natural tendency to put people into categories of haves and have-nots based on biases. Really it is a matter of our identity and how we define others through a secular view defined by our individual biases.

Biblically speaking, our identity is not bound by our sex, race, nationality, sexual orientation, or any other manner in which society wants to define us. Galatians 3:27–29 says, "For as many of you as were baptized into Christ have put on Christ. There is neither Jew nor Greek, there is neither slave nor free, there is no male and female, for you are all one in Christ Jesus. And if you are Christ's, then you are Abraham's offspring, heirs according to promise."

Thankfully identity, through the lens of faith in Jesus, is not about one's status in society, but instead about the unity we have with an all-powerful God. As soon as we are justified in Christ, we take on a new identity, which is "by faith in the Son of God, who loved me and gave himself for me" (Galatians 2:20). The security in knowing that our identity as Christians is found in Christ is that we trust that it will not change and that the world does not have any influence over our identity.

This can be difficult, yet it is essential as Christians to reconcile, as otherwise when someone tells us we are "nonessential" regardless of the circumstances, it will generate an emotional response, and we will get consumed and place our worth in a category detrimental to our health. Identity when found in Christ allows us to live above the microlevel of emotional influence.

When I think of identity and what we are attempting to forge in our lives, I think of my late acquaintance, Pastor Ken Hutcherson. I can remember vividly the first time a pastor preached on the high priestly prayer that Jesus prays in John 17:1–19. It was in 2013 and was a message shared by Pastor Hutcherson at my church's annual pastors conference. It was the most influential message I had ever heard in person up to that point.

Some may remember Pastor Hutcherson as Ken Hutcherson, NFL football player with the Cowboys and the Seahawks, or Pastor Hutch, as many in Seattle and around the world know him. He played in the NFL for several years, but that was not where he placed his identity. He was the lead pastor of Antioch Bible Church in Seattle. Playing professional football was simply a useful platform to get Pastor Hutch in front of people to share the gospel. His identity came from his relationship and unity with Jesus Christ.

What I remember vividly about that night was how he could barely walk up five stairs to get to the top level where he would preach and how he had to constantly wipe away the uncontrollable fluids that ran from his nostrils. He struggled with the stairs and the body fluids because he was in the final stage of prostate cancer, of which he lived with for ten years. It was about three months after I heard him speak that Pastor Hutch passed away and joined Jesus as a saint in heaven. In the high priestly prayer, in addition to praying for himself and his disciples, it is for us that Jesus prayed and for all who choose to go the way of Jesus.

An important lesson for me—and I trust you too—comes through this message of unity and hope found in the high priestly prayer.

It is natural for us getting back from a deployment to want to reintegrate back into our homes, our families, our work, and whatever else we may have going on. But the challenge with that after a deployment is that we inevitably have changed, and in this change, sometimes our identity can shift unintentionally. In this, we can be the last to admit that we have changed.

And as I separated from the deployment where my spiritual discipline was as strong as it has ever been, I lost focus on spiritual disciplines, causing me to lose focus of my identity. The biggest challenge from the reintegration for me was separating my identity of being a husband, father, president of Impact Montana, and employee at the VA from my identity as an army chaplain. In my experience, I have found that part of our reintegration issues can stem from an identity crisis.

The world will draw us toward placing our identity in these things instead of in our relationship with Jesus. Even placing my identity in my role as a chaplain instead of being a child of the King proved to be unhealthy. What gets me out of this challenge most often is being convicted that being a husband, father, and so forth is not where I place my security, hope, or identity because knowing myself as well as I do, I know that I fail and will continue to fail.

When we place our identity in the unity and relationship we have with Jesus, we receive an overwhelming comfort knowing that we don't have to be perfect or anything else that the world wants

to define us by. My encouragement is to not place your identity in what you do, who you are married to, what you drive, how big your house is, and so forth, but instead the hope you have and the relationship and unity you have with Jesus.

We live in a world that promotes competition and separation from the pack, resulting in identity based on accomplishment and biases. Identity for us as Christians is not about what we have done, but instead by what has been done for us. We mustn't lose sight of that.

CHAPTER 4

THRIVING

IN 2014 WHEN I STARTED the nonprofit Impact Montana, on the programming side of the organization we established six pillars that we deemed essential in the role of supporting our Montana service members, vets, and their families. These wellness pillars were primarily based on factors that were recognized as being influential in one's ability to successfully integrate back into civilian life after either an active-duty career or coming back from a deployment as a guardsman or reservist.

We intended to develop programs that would align with each of the pillars and fill essential gaps in services and support. For example, in the social wellness pillar, the intent was to create a social construct that would allow veterans to gather with their peers and go on extensive recreational journeys to reestablish the bond that had been missed since being in the military. Great idea, right? Others found this to be a great idea as well.

Thankfully about two years later and prior to this program being in effect, we had been introduced to another Montana nonprofit that was doing this exact thing and doing it very well, so we did not pursue this specific program primarily because we did not have the margin to be able to start something this extensive at the time. And now several years later we have

several programs promoting the same recreation therapy for healing.

Another example of a program we had explored based on needs was programming to support the effort of placing and training a dog with a veteran in need of medical support, a service dog program. Just like the recreational program concept, service dog connection and training programs started to get developed, therefore limiting our role to being a referral hub to those needing services.

A significant amount of our value comes in sharing these opportunities with veterans who would benefit from these legitimate organizations, not duplicating services that other organizations support well.

Well is the keyword. The Montana Veterans Program, K9Care Montana, and Dog Tag Buddies are excellent examples of organizations that are operating in Montana, doing things very well. I have tremendous respect for the leaders in these organizations who share the same type of passion that I do when it comes to our work. I think that mutual passion allows us to see the common good of being able to work well together as a team.

In our years of operating, we have committed to not duplicating what other organizations are doing well. Instead we are the referral and advocate for individuals to leverage other programs.

Despite the favor of these pillars and what appeared to be an effectively developing mechanism of support, after my most recent deployment, I found out just how relevant and effective the Impact Montana model actually is. And because of its relevance, we have changed the simplicity of the language and intention from having independent wellness pillars to collectively serving as "veteran thrive factors."

The significance of the change is predominantly from my experience honing in on each thrive factor and targeting the means that contribute to one's personal ability to thrive spiritually. Thriving in general means different things to different people; however, in this case, we are going to put thriving in the context of thriving spiritually.

> *Gold Nugget: Thriving is about the energy produced when an individual and/or family can leverage the things in their lives that are most valuable to them and managing them through a faith-based lens, making all of it purposeful.*

WHY THRIVE FACTORS

I mentioned that initially our intent with Impact Montana was to develop programs that accommodate the needs of our service members, veterans, and their families. The more I dissected each factor and their relation to each other based on my own wants, needs, desires, the more I realized that my ability to be at my optimal functioning level was based on the wellness pillars collectively, working together as a holistic model for personal wellness but perceived through the lens of faith.

The concept of holistic wellness is starting to become trendy, and models will vary, often including mental health and intellectual wellness in them. However, because Impact Montana committed early on to not investing in mental or emotional health services, not because we don't think they are important facets of health, but primarily because the idea was for our other pillars to promote sound mental and emotional health naturally. In this, we support and allow government health agencies and other nonprofit organizations to continue spearheading the effort of improving mental and emotional health through specific programming.

In the case of intellectual health, we categorize that with the career wellness thrive factor, knowing and understanding that someone who is growing intellectually will be benefiting vocationally and through other aspects of life relative to career.

Because life is more than just about work, making and managing money, who you know, and family dynamics, I started to recognize that the propensity to thrive or be influential was predicated upon proactivity and intentional focus in managing life's stress. Even without challenges or stress, with all the undue pressure we place on ourselves and that society places on us, it is difficult to thrive. If you are not thriving, it is impossible to make an impact.

As we continued to move forward organizationally, I found that working with returning veterans and the challenges they had faced during military service were making it very difficult to be at the top of their game consistently. This was hard to fathom because service members are used to living at a high functional capacity consistently; however, this was not the case once out of service for many of the individuals I was working with and walking alongside of.

Consistently functioning at a high level, or thriving, separates someone who is chasing impact, or living in impact, from someone who is bogged down by life's circumstances to include what has happened to them and the inability to manage the repercussions of the circumstances.

In many cases, the spiritual health, specifically perspective, will allow someone to grasp the concept that what has happened to them is largely uncontrollable, but how they respond to it is within the realm of their control.

I believe that a big turning point in our organization's story is this "aha" moment of taking all of our wellness pillars and meshing them together as being mutually inclusive factors of one's ability to get back to this high level, or optimal functioning, instead of just saying that if we have programs under these categories, individuals and families will benefit. And when I think of thriving, I think of positive energy, or a spiritual force for good, not only in the individual but that energy transferring to others. I naturally correlate thriving to the pursuit of something great, soul purpose, and essentially impact. Being in tune to the thrive factors, whether a veteran or not, increases our energy, which means we have more energy to influence others.

At the end of the day, the vitality of the thrive factors comes from having a purposed pursuit in each of these wellness categories so the individual can execute the strategy to achieve the vision. And because pursuit of a larger vision (macrolevel) for the benefit of others is paramount in one's ability to live in impact, it is important to also pursue what helps a person thrive on an individual scale and at a microlevel. Without a strategy to thrive according to the vision, the energy is either not available or unsustainable.

While the thrive factor model consists of six thrive factors, each factor has associated components that determine what develops the optimal comprehensive wellness. Thrive factors create a natural mechanism for personal accountability and a framework for managing expectations according to God's desire for our lives in various areas, including marriage, parenting, health, and how we spend our time making a living, socially as well as financially. It is your prescription to mutually align desires with God's desires in these areas.

COMPREHENSIVE WELLNESS ASSESSMENT

"The unexamined life is not worth living" (attributed to Socrates).

Once these wellness pillars self-identified as a holistic solution to one's ability to thrive, they became purposeful, with the purpose including to breed self-awareness and strategy development from things where energy is derived and are valued by the individual.

Without this purpose, we get lost in the societal conditioning of everything but thriving. If we are not thriving, we are not being influential, let alone chasing impact. The results of massive amounts of stress, the dependency on technology, standard automation, and societal addictions, to name a few, lead us down a long road disconnected from our purpose. Our optimal solution is to apply purpose and biblical reasoning to everything we do, promoting the intention and focus to identify what exactly we are chasing, and how we are going to get there and sustain impact once we have reached it.

Even though there is an established list of thrive factors, there is no standard prescription for someone to thrive. What supports my ability to thrive is going to look vastly different than anyone else's, including my own family members. Just as there are no fingerprints alike, our prescription to thrive is also unique. Unlike our prescription to thrive, one commonality we all have is that we all will face adversity or go through some sort of suffering.

> *Gold Nugget: The propensity to thrive or be influential through adversity is predicated upon the perceived value of the adversity. This recognized value affords someone the ability to create opportunity when without the recognition of the value, the opportunity is limited.*

Everyone has challenges. There is not one person who has walked on the face of the earth who has been without them, including Jesus. The value may not be recognized until after the fact as it is often difficult to see the sun in the middle of the storm, but the sun is always there, and there is always value as a result of adversity.

When we are engaged in a holistic model of thriving, putting purpose toward our wellness, the thrive factors put focus on opportunity, opportunity to get rid of toxicity, align with values, create margin, and produce increased amounts of energy based on wants, needs, purpose, and so forth. It is certainly possible to be outside the purview of our purpose, which decreases the likeliness of thriving.

There are always things to give up in exchange for something else because we have a finite amount of time, space, and resources. And looking at the big picture, or all of the thrive factors as one big puzzle, it becomes clear which puzzle pieces (individual components of the thrive factors) offer increased energy and which ones do not.

As I have found in working with individuals and families gauging alignment with factors of spiritual health, it is easier to identify toxicities that need to be eliminated and factors needing to replace the toxins when the perspective is clear. If the perspective is unclear, then it is more difficult to recognize where one is attempting to go and what factors in the thrive factor model will actually promote thriving.

The intention in assessing the thrive factors is to build a comprehensive framework to support one's ability to thrive or be at one's functional capacity based on margin availability or operating at an excess of capacity, which we can attribute to energy management. We all operate below or at our max capacity, and the awareness of which level we are operating is an integral part of developing the comprehensive framework for maximizing energy. It is the assessment of various contributing factors to each thrive factor itself that evaluates and identifies the optimal solution to assist in operating at functional capacity.

SERVING OTHERS

It is no secret that we can't serve others optimally without being at our functional capacity. Impact can be limited, despite intent to operate in purpose due to mismanagement of energy. And it is not always easy to recognize when we are not operating proficiently or at our functional capacity.

This hits very close to home for me as I had a very good friend who I shared time with supporting Montana veterans. He was a tremendous asset in this effort. Normally this would not be a big deal, but after I had returned from my deployment to Afghanistan, I had noticed that he had a severe downward shift in his health and wellness. In the ten months that I was gone, his physical health went extremely downhill, the stress level at work increased tremendously, and I noticed his social life changed as well, influencing his ability to thrive as he had been used to doing.

As we visited about these things on a drive across the state upon my return, his downward shift was to the point that I told him I did not want to be officiating his funeral but that I feared it was heading that way. The out-of-balance physical health and career stress had put him over his functional capacity. A man who would give the shirt off his back to anyone had lost the energy to metaphorically be able to even take a shirt off his back. Unfortunately, less than eight months after our conversation, I was presiding over his funeral.

Serving others as a facet of spiritual health should naturally produce energy for us, especially when the service is something we are deeply connected or called to do. I get tremendously energized when I have the opportunity to serve others. I notice that if I miss an opportunity to serve or contribute to someone else's life, my energy depletes. But I can also notice a negative effect when I am overtaxed in serving others because another factor, like quality time with my family, contributes to my ability to thrive being compromised.

It is important to note that if we are not cognizant of what our thrive factors are or the things that positively contribute to our energy and overall impact, there is a tendency to rely on others to determine our own ability to thrive. Because relying on others to influence our comprehensive wellness is outside the scope of our control, there is no direct connection in understanding what gives us positive energy, ultimately leaving us void of that energy needed to thrive. The ability to thrive is a direct result of our self-awareness and provides us energy and connects us to pursuing our soul purpose.

Generally, men and women in the military function at their optimal level, or functional capacity, which helps them advance in rank and achieve greater responsibilities. Often the adrenaline rush as a result of military service contributes positively to one's ability to sustain their energy; however, once the individual separates from service, the adrenaline decreases, and the reality of life outside the military sets in, challenges often begin, as does the need to reassess the comprehensive wellness.

Again, self-awareness and goal orientation based on energy management relative to one's soul purpose helps to promote spiritual maturity and the ability to thrive and live in impact.

THRIVE FACTOR 1: SPIRITUAL HEALTH

"For those who live according to the flesh set their minds on the things of the flesh, but those who live according to the Spirit set their minds on the things of the Spirit" (Romans 8:5).

When I think of one's ability to thrive, I think first and foremost of living inside of purpose. We all have purpose and meaning and a reason for being here, but we don't all have the recognition of purpose or meaning because we choose to not seek them from a relationship with God. My objective is to live out this mission by giving God what he desires, which means the thrive factors, and the energy derived will point toward God's glory.

Because we have been created with purpose, to be something greater than who we believe we are, and our gifts, skill, abilities, and perception are all contributing factors to who we actually are or who God says we are, doesn't it make sense to maximize our opportunity for giving glory to God by recognizing and living in our purpose according to him?

> *Gold Nugget: The source of our perception, our hope, the grace we don't deserve, and the love we receive has the power to change the trajectory of our lives.*

This innate purpose separates us from every other species that has ever existed. When we understand this, it changes everything. We go from thinking our self-identified purpose or self-defined faith saves us to realizing that faith has little to do with us and everything to do with what God has done for us through Jesus.

In observations made of professing Christians, I have found that often faith is about how people think they are contributing toward their salvation, where salvation comes at the moment one's heart is turned toward God and professing that there is nothing we can do because Jesus as God's Son has already done everything for us. It bears repeating that faith has little to do with us and everything to do with God. We either accept or deny what God has done, continues to do, and will do by our willingness to prayerfully align with his will for us.

Perspective and spiritual health provide an incredible opportunity in that everything we do can give credence to God's glory. This is how our spiritual health drives our actions and contributions in life. It is my belief through God's Word and my experience that thriving personally and living in impact starts here!

MY JOURNEY, GOD'S STORY

Just after a few short years of joining the Army National Guard, I found myself in what scholars call the cradle of civilization, or Mesopotamia, involved in a personal conflict of attempting to understand good versus evil. And not being a student of the Bible at the time, I was introduced to the fact that Abraham, the father of the Christian faith, was born in the immediate area we were serving in.

But despite growing up in various churches and having an understanding of who God is and who Jesus was, my heart had never been invested in living for God. So to be serving in this distinct area, I felt a tug on my heart to change my ways to align more with what I understood to be a representation of what a Christian looks like.

Unfortunately this only held form while I was in Iraq. When I came back to the States, there was a natural transition back to pursuing things that were of value to me (mostly pleasure) and away from this faith and trust in God. I went back to a fast-paced life that was all about me. The faith proved to be about my shallow understanding of God and me being able to fit him into a box that was convenient for me.

The conflict of good versus evil had gone from being involved in a physical battle of oppositional forces to being a spiritual battle internally of oppositional forces. And for several months, I pursued nothing but things that felt good to me or filled my pleasure tank. Everything after my deployment became about me because I felt like I was owed something.

The more I chased pleasure, the more my life was spinning out of control despite it not looking like it to other people. There was no discipline, accountability, or baseline of which I was living my life. It was all based on pleasure until I received my wake-up call from God.

In the midst of some internal struggles that were starting to be identified, a friend gave me a copy of Rick Warren's *Purpose-Driven Life.* Thinking I knew something about purpose, this book opened my eyes and heart to a whole new recognition of purpose for life. Unfortunately the hold that my fleshly desires and the world had on me was stronger than the new perspective that was starting to be developed, until God orchestrated an introduction to someone who showed me what this purpose-driven life looked like.

A gathering of what was supposed to be just some guy friends hanging out at one of our houses turned out to be the occasion that I met my wife. Angie was an anomaly for me in that she was faith-focused and did not compromise on her values for personal gain or pleasure. It did not take me long to recognize that God was working in my life and that she was an answer to prayer.

Once I committed my life to following Jesus at the tail end of 2005, the burden of my past and the trajectory of my future had changed. Aspects of my life that once were incredibly important became minute. There was the beginning of a shift in my inability to manage life's circumstances to allow God to direct and guide my path in life. For the first time in my life, purpose was prioritized over pleasure, resulting in a significant perspective change.

I share this story, not because it is unique, but because it is common. It is God's. Reconciliation back to God is not about what I did, but what he did for us, specifically sending his Son Jesus Christ to atone for our sins. No goodness we can offer will satisfy the requirements for reconciliation of man with God; however, God satisfied that requirement through his Son Jesus's death on the cross, burial, and resurrection.

When we recognize and revere that God has the desire for us to be aligned to his will, that Jesus Christ is the Son of God, and that he came to live as God in human flesh and died a sinless death for our sins so we could spend eternity with God in heaven and not be damned to eternal separation from God, it is life-changing.

SPIRITUAL WELLNESS ASSESSMENT

When I think of spiritual wellness and our ability to thrive, I can't help but think of a buoy in the water and the buoy's ability to always be at the top of the water surface. Sometimes the water is calm, with no boat chop or weather affecting its smoothness. It is certainly less common to experience smooth water than it is choppy water, which parallels our lives.

Now if that water gets a little choppy from boats or the weather, that buoy still has a function. It still has purpose. It may not always be at the top of the surface, but because of its attributes, it will recover and fulfill its purpose as intended. I would reasonably say that this is mostly how life is represented. The buoy is always going to perform its function based on the character of the water at any given point.

A spiritually fit person—that is, they understand life's meaning, are connected to soul purpose according to biblical principles, have an understanding of love and grace received from God, and living a joyous and hopeful life—is not bound to society's moral fluidity and is engaged in spiritual disciplines, for constant growth is similar to the buoy.

Regardless of the type of precarious situation or stress one finds themselves in, a spiritually well individual continues to thrive despite the circumstances. Conditions are irrelevant to this individual, just like it is to the buoy.

With this theory, we can add to it the notion that perspective brings some relativity to the conversation. For example, someone who lives in Boston, Chicago, San Diego, or any large metropolitan area, for example, will have differing perspectives from someone living in rural America or, in much of Montana's case, frontier America.

Despite these perspective differences, the assessment of their spiritual health remains the same. The components of spiritual wellness are based on God's truth and are absolute. There is no relativity when it comes to love, hope, purpose, equality, liberty, justice, identity, morality, and so forth. And misrepresenting anything that God has ordained as absolute is a detriment to our spiritual wellness.

To continue with the metaphors, an individual not spiritually attuned to God's truth is like a rock. No matter what happens with the rock or its size, shape, or smoothness, it will fall to the floor of the body of water eventually. Again, a rock is a rock, and its ability to perform like a buoy is impossible. It will perform as a rock despite the circumstances and characteristics of the water it finds itself in. It is not optimal to be like a rock when it comes to our spiritual health.

If we look at some of the circumstances we may find ourselves in like addiction, trauma, loss or death of a loved one, or loss of occupation, the individual with the buoy-like spiritual resilience will be able to recover quicker, unlike someone without hope or the understanding of God's love and mercy, a disconnect from purpose, and a misaligned identity, who will struggle to find their way through the circumstances they find themselves in.

What formulates our spiritual wellness and frankly our ability to float versus sink is our comprehension of who God is based on his holy Word and connection to the Holy Spirit, the authority of the spiritual realm. God is the master formulator of soul purpose, hope, love, forgiveness, and all things spiritual. I submit to you that the difference between plain living and thriving is based on one's connection to these facets of God's formula for life. Not only do we live in a physical world, but we also live in a spiritual world, and we all have access to the creator of both.

Along with the aforementioned absolute truths, another strong indicator of our spiritual wellness is our understanding of grace, or forgiveness. We are all flawed individuals who need forgiveness, but all may not recognize the nature of forgiveness. Along with love, it is the most powerful offer given to all by God through the blood of Christ. And just like love, there is no condition in which we can align with in order to have access to it. We are not to forgive and love others only based on satisfying conditions. We are to forgive and love others because it is commanded of us and offered to us from God.

Without a connection to God, our spiritual health is compromised, and we end up going through life seeking internal instead of eternal desires, essentially pleasure instead of purpose. And seeking pleasure over purpose minimizes one's ability to thrive and at the same time live in impact.

PLEASURE VERSUS PURPOSE

I continue to reflect on my story, but it really is no different than a large portion of our society in that prior to having the recognition that my life is relevant outside of how much money I have, who I am married to, what my career is, or what kind of car I drive, I chased pleasure. Society tends to define us by our socioeconomic status, which promotes filling this definition through chasing pleasure until the value of purpose is greater than the perceived value of pleasure. The fact of the matter is that one will never find purpose living in pleasure.

> *Gold Nugget: Patience reveals purpose, and the time lost not living in impact relative to the time living in pursuit of pleasure is opportunity lost.*

Perhaps this is why many people go through a midlife crisis. They realize that what they have done is not satisfying, so they seek additional pleasure to fill that void. Filling a pleasure void with pleasure only creates deeper despair.

Another consideration to make in regard to pleasure is that when we are caught up in life's stressful circumstances, we tend to compromise on perspective because we are too wrapped up in how we are going to meet the need of filling our pleasure tank. We only see or pursue the things that are going to feel good, which is giving into our fleshly desires and, in reality, a barrier to our spiritual health as well as physical health and other thrive factors.

NOT ABOUT US

I don't think I can hit on this point enough, so it bears repeating: impact is bigger than you or I. Don't fall victim to thinking it is only about you because that is where we get into trouble. If we are overinflated in thinking we are doing well, we will shut others off with arrogance, and if we are underinflated, we will not seek help when needed. There is a margin between what our natural capacity for impact is and what our spiritual capacity is, so praying and trusting that God will reveal opportunities is beneficial to our spiritual health.

One of my biggest personal flaws that has been revealed in the last couple of years is that I have a tendency, like most people, whether they are Christian or not, to think I can handle things on my own when life gets chaotic. I naturally start to neglect my relationship with God, and it is quick to show. So important facets of spiritual health like contributing to spiritual gifts, living in character strengths, or now focusing on the thrive factors get neglected, and stress increases faster than if I am pointedly praying and slowing down enough to align with these facets of spiritual health. Again, this is evidence of our natural capacity having a drastically lower capacity than our spiritual capacity and the capacity that involves significant assistance from God.

Relying on ourselves and limiting God's capabilities in our lives will provide enough room for oppositional forces to scheme us into thinking we are the ones responsible for making an impact, when we ultimately fall victim to the pride of life and lust of the flesh (1 John 2:16). The spiritual battles and warfare occurring in our culture and from the world, our own sin nature, and Satan are enough to warrant daily prayer for spiritual protection with the armor of God (Ephesians 6:10–18).

The difference in thinking we can navigate life on our own is seen in the limitations and importance of perspective as it relates to our spiritual health. The limitations are revealed in the behavior of children as a derivative of spiritual immaturity as well as in adults who are spiritually immature. You cannot expect a child to understand meaning, purpose, hope, and identity, but you can expect an adult to have a general recognition of it or at least grasp a concept of it through a secular lens.

It is from my experience working with both individuals and families of faith and without faith that perspective and understanding the significance of Jesus's miracle birth, sinless life, death on the cross, burial, and resurrection from the tomb shifts one's perspective from being selfish to selfless, from seeking pleasure to seeking purpose, and from having challenges with identity to pursuing Christlikeness. This shift in perspective is powerful and in fact life-changing. This is the unique nature of the chaplaincy, having the ability to work with believers and nonbelievers alike, and individuals who are on different spectrums of spiritual maturity. It is a beautiful thing.

And spiritual awakening, occurring from the point that we recognize that Jesus Christ is the Son of God, that without him our capacity is much lower, and that we are weaker than we are with him by our side, we experience spiritual maturation. Growth comes when we use the aforementioned spiritual gifts, when we are living in our character strengths and focused on thriving. In this, we are in the midst of blessing God and others instead of ourselves. This is the point we know we are spiritually alive and thriving.

SPIRITUAL LETHARGY

The opposite of thriving in many cases is lethargy, and being lethargic, or without spiritual energy, is certainly a point that no one who has experienced being spiritually alive wants to feel. Thus, having the proactive means to fight the battle of spiritual lethargy is vital in our defense posture.

Having worked with soldiers of all walks of life, including atheists, LDS, Catholics, and evangelicals, I have realized that there are common impediments that will get in the way of our faith, which have the propensity to breed spiritual lethargy. Some of the challenges we face include the three we already mentioned (the world, our sin nature, and Satan), along with a misunderstanding of the character of God and naïveté of the existence of evil, often coming from a lack of biblical instruction or interpretation.

The misunderstanding of who God is remains self-explanatory yet is something that gets revealed often. But what does not get revealed all that often, primarily because it is not a typical discussion, is the difference between good and evil, especially in the context that evil exists, but it might not be in the form that we would reason to believe it exists. Just like the fact that we will never completely comprehend God's goodness, we will never begin to completely fathom the power of evil and the spiritual warfare that is prevalent in our world.

It is impossible to have an intimate relationship with God

and understanding of these things without having an intimate relationship with the Bible. The Bible is where God has articulated who he is and the breadth of the spiritual battles that man has faced since the garden. It is vital we go to the Bible if we want to know who God is and why he wants a relationship with us.

I want to clarify two points before we move on.

1. The spiritual energy, whether it is weak or mighty, is not a salvation issue. Romans 10:9–10 reminds us that once we faithfully abide in Jesus Christ, he will be with us always. Spiritual lethargy may set in, largely in part because of evil schemes, but remaining true to biblical spiritual disciplines like prayer, worship, Bible study, serving, fellowship, discipleship, and fasting (1 Timothy 4:7) will keep us closely connected to God and strong in our faith.

2. The set of thrive factors is simply a list of areas in life that have proven to be difficult to proactively manage for many. In my experience with solution-focused counseling, the objective is to help an individual self-identify optimal solutions for a challenge that they are going through and to get back on course with goals and objectives from their prescription to thrive. Staying in tune, through a faith-based lens, to what helps someone thrive is a reasonable approach to change poor patterns of thought and behavior.

THRIVE FACTOR 2: PHYSICAL HEALTH

"Do you not know that in a race all the runners run, but only one receives the prize? So, run that you may obtain it" (1 Corinthians 9:24).

In the latter part of the summer of 2018, as I was going on my typical morning run in Afghanistan, a young male soldier (whom we will call PV2) was running ahead of me by himself. The fact that he was by himself was motivation for me to catch him and join him on his run.

As I caught up to him, I started to have a conversation, hoping it would help him take his mind off running. I could tell by the way he was struggling that running was not his thing, but it was something he was being mandated to do because he was a soldier. I was particularly intrigued because this was an individual whom I did not know but was feeling a tug on my heart to get to hear part of his story that morning. Something about this situation was not usual.

I ended up joining PV2 for his entire five-mile run, but it wasn't the run itself that was memorable. It was our conversation. It was the connection made on that morning. I would like to think that our conversation and connection proved to be valuable to him. And I trust that this was the case because of his demeanor every time I saw him after that run and the personal invitation he sent to me to join him for his promotion later on in the deployment.

The beauty of his eventual promotion is that because of PV2's less than desirable (by army standards) physical conditioning, he was actually demoted to private second class, an E-2, either before or during the initial part of the deployment. And because of that, he was adamant about getting out of the army. PV2 was done. But something hit him in the deployment that put him on the path of being promoted to specialist (E-4) in a matter of months and taking advantage of his time in Afghanistan.

Two parts of our conversation during the run really hit home for me.

1. As we were starting out and after I introduced myself to him, I started to paint a blank canvas with his story. As a young soldier and through conversation, I quickly recognized that he was not unlike many of the soldiers whom I have worked with in the past that struggled mightily with purpose and meaning. As we were running, I proceeded to paint this canvas with questions related to his service and reason for running. The response during the run was that he was doing it because he was forced to do it. He was demoted and on the verge of being kicked out of the army if his physical

fitness did not improve. But rather than do it because it was good for him, PV2 was doing it because someone else was motivating him. He was mandated to do it.

While we ran together, I started to challenge him to reapply his reason for running, to become a distinct purpose, to give it meaning, more than just because he had to. And as we continued to engage in dialogue, it felt to me like things were clicking. The conversation about spiritual health and being able to connect purpose to everything he did, including things he did not like to do, became spiritual, or purposeful. It brought on a whole new perspective for him. And from my purview, this resonated throughout the rest of the deployment, changing his demeanor and energy.

2. I also remember vividly that on our last mile, when things really got difficult and he wanted to stop, I distracted him. In the Army Resilience Training world, this is called *Mental Games*. Essentially I distracted him by doing the alphabet city game. We started at A to list cities progressively, all the way to Z. Before we knew it, the five-mile run had been completed.

I tell this story for the same reason I have and will continue to share some personal stories throughout this book. There is tremendous value in witnessing when someone's perspective shifts from doing things they think they should be doing, such as conforming to what the world says they should be doing, to thriving based on connection to a perceived purpose.

The challenge for PV2 (now a Specialist in the US Army) and many others is that when they are taken away from the hardship or the focus of navigating through the hardship with purpose or intent, there is susceptibility to defaulting back to being pleasure-centric individuals.

We forfeit the desire to stay on the course of impact because we have become accustomed to doing things the easy way and frankly the way that fills our pleasure tanks.

MY JOURNEY PURSUING PHYSICAL WELLNESS

Thriving physically for me has been one of the tougher challenges I have faced in my life. And if I am being honest, it is predicated on growing up with little boundaries established by my parents, eating for pleasure, and having no limits.

The one time in my life that there could be an indication of thriving physically was when I was in Iraq for my first deployment and as physically active as I had ever been. There had been various periods in my life that physical fitness was a priority; however, the priority was based on the security found in physique, or maybe lack of security would be more accurate to say.

My pursuit for being physically fit was based on wanting to feel better because of looking better, not because I was actually healthier. So the changes needing to be healthier as a result of a diet change were missing. I continued to live in the same patterns I had my entire life not recognizing that nutrition was a primary component to physical health and the holistic balance to provide what I have found to be true security.

In this out-of-balance approach to physical health, I found myself with a variety of issues. Immediately after my first deployment, I started experiencing very low energy and chronic fatigue. I also noticed my cognitive processing suffered in times of increased stress. Not to mention I had unusual amounts of pain in my joints for being under thirty years old. I was twenty-seven years old and experiencing what seventy-year-olds notoriously go through. Plainly stated, I was miserable.

While attempting to identify what was going on, my primary doctor recommended I stop all high-impact sports. This meant no racquetball, basketball, and running. I was in the Army National Guard for goodness sakes, and running is a part of our physical fitness test. How could I not run and stay in the organization?

Needless to say, I struggled with this. This was a period that

I just accepted the fact that this was the way it was going to be. The struggle continued for about eight years despite some pretty significant nutritional changes, I still battled with these issues.

In these eight years, I stepped on a scale at a health fair that calculated biological age. Most of the individuals who had stepped on the scale were unpleasantly surprised by the results of their measurement, sometimes upwards of twenty to thirty years older than the actual age of the individual. I was hesitant to do this mostly because of others' results, regardless of the fact that my physical conditioning was not all that much perceivably worse than many at the fair.

But when I got on the scale and after it had time to calculate my results, I was shocked. I wasn't biologically twenty or even thirty years older than my real age. I was forty years older biologically than my actual age.

This was genuinely the first time that I became concerned with my health. After all, if my biological age were in the early seventies and the average age of a male at death was the late seventies, I was, in theory, biologically in the last seven years of my life. This will wake most thirty-some-year-olds up from a health slumber, and it certainly did me.

What I came to find out after all of these years is that my poor habits, and frankly addiction to sugar, had contributed mightily to all of these issues. Life had been somewhat hard on my body with sports, the military, and other recreational activities, but I certainly did not help myself with the amount of sugar I regularly consumed. In fact, this is such a big challenge for me that I often find myself telling people who I am discussing addiction with that if there were a sugar addiction center, I would be the first one standing in line attempting to detox. Sugar has been a struggle most of my life and is more formidable of a threat to my health than alcohol or any drug. It is that bad.

Leading up to my second deployment, it wasn't necessarily the pain and fatigue that was still a concern. It was my brain's ability to manage stress. Just like after my first deployment, I was finding consistent challenges with my brain's ability to function, and it intensified as the stress in my life increased.

In visiting with a neuropsychologist and after completing a neuro-psych evaluation, I was given three options to help with the focus and stress management. The doc did not diagnose me with ADHD but proceeded to tell me that my challenges were in the ADHD family and that there were options for me to help with the ability to focus and manage stress. Had I actually been diagnosed with ADHD, it would have deemed me ineligible to deploy to that theatre of operations, so I was thankful that this was not the case.

My intention for this deployment was not to deploy with this inability to manage my cognition or handle increased amounts of stress. The stress was inevitable, but what was not inevitable was how my brain and body would respond as a result of attempting to manage it appropriately. The three options that the doctor gave me were to:

1. Go on prescription medication on an as-needed basis.
2. Try neurofeedback for six months prior to the deployment.
3. Make a concentrated effort to manage my nutrition with increased healthy fats, protein, and amino acids and little to no sugar and food dye–induced foods.

I was appreciative of the options given to me and not the limitation of just the medication as my only option. I had no idea at the time how big of an issue food dye (namely red) is and how widespread it is in our food system.

I was certainly intrigued with the neurofeedback primarily because I had researched it in the past and it posed as the easiest, yet most expensive, therapy for my brain and transitioning from the challenges I had in the past to where I wanted to be functionally. But because I would have to drive a hundred miles both ways weekly for the six months, it just was not feasible.

The first option of prescription medication was not the option of choice based on the personal desire to avoid pharmaceuticals as much as possible, so diet it was. The simple advice of eating healthy fats in the morning and balancing out proteins with the consumed carbs seemed reasonable enough. The doctor even went as far as encouraging me to add protein to my daily afternoon caffeine to aid in energy management and support brain function. With the brain health perceivably improving and pain also somewhat improving, I started the process of reshaping my holistic health in preparation for the deployment.

This is when I was encouraged to try biofeedback. I knew what neurofeedback was, but the concept of hooking up to a computer and running a body systems function check to neutralize less than desirable facets of my health was foreign.

I was convinced that this was something worth trying, and because I helped service members and veterans get connected to natural and complementary therapies, it was in my best interest to experience the therapy so I could understand how it worked and share my experience with those who may benefit from it.

The investment made was worth much more than the cost. In my series of biofeedback visits, it was determined that I had significant gut health issues (as a result of my lifetime of poor diet choices) leading to vast inflammation in the body. And inflammation was in fact leading to the majority of the pain I had experienced in the past and still had not completely reduced. Not only that, but I had learned in the process that gut health is a contributing promoter to the brain's ability to function after having started listening to Dr. Amen's *Brain Warrior's Way* podcasts on Brain Health.

By focusing on more than just masking the symptoms like had been done in the past, leading up to the second deployment, I felt I was finally getting to a place physically that would afford me the opportunity to be of the highest value for those I was serving with. It would also allow me to set some pretty lofty goals not only for myself, but to challenge members of our battalion in Afghanistan as well. For the first time in my life, I was starting to thrive physically because I was applying purpose in my pursuit to thrive.

DEPLOYMENT GOALS

We all have events that are identified as big, life-altering events, with the potential to challenge us in ways we have never been challenged before. Whether it is a marathon or trek through the Bob Marshall Wilderness in our case here in Montana, it is important to test our moxie, endurance, and especially resilience. My Afghanistan deployment was this event for me, at this stage in my life, the event to challenge me to the core—spiritually, physically, and emotionally.

Unlike many deployments, this one offered a little bit less of a challenge due to the nature of our mission, to support the operating environment with logistics management. While we were scattered throughout the theatre of operations, our role was strictly management of commodities and contract personnel, which meant threat or danger was limited relative to other operations.

In the months prior to this deployment, some peers in the unit and I started discussing some potential unit physical fitness challenge ideas. The one specific goal I had in mind was to run 495 miles because our unit designation was the 495th Combat Sustainment Support Battalion. If nothing else, I was going to literally hit the ground running, and in the nine months with boots in Afghanistan, I was going to make my best attempt to accomplish this feat. And because I knew the value in this goal, I wanted to have my peers join me to develop some camaraderie, or *esprit de corps*.

As I had found in the past unintentionally, compromising on health and what is consumed means compromise on the body's ability to maximize its performance. The older you get, the easier it is to recognize there is less room for compromise.

A friend and fitness advocate who I have worked with

professionally in the military risk reduction and resilience world likes to use the metaphor of putting high-quality oil into a car and specifically not anything that would limit performance. This is exactly what we do when we don't think about our bodies being high-performance machines and how we are taking for granted the systems designed to function more proficiently than the way we treat them.

In order for me to accomplish the physical fitness goals that I set out to accomplish, I had to maximize the compromise of eating typical dining facility food to help me thrive in the face of adversity. The compromise was maximized by ordering high-quality *Isagenix* food-based and nutrition-dense supplements from the States throughout our premobilization training and the deployment itself.

The end result was finishing my extracurricular goals and the 495 miles on the second-to-last day we were supposed to be in Afghanistan because of the focused pursuit of the goals. I had successfully completed the physical fitness goals I had set out to accomplish, and it felt good.

Of course, if I had not set out to accomplish these goals and hold myself accountable by measuring progress weekly relative to the end goals, it would have been very difficult to achieve the target. Part of chasing impact is having the target for impact, the vision of what you want to accomplish, what it will take to get there, and, most importantly, the why, or purpose, for reaching the destination. I also had the available margin to manage the goals successfully.

POST-DEPLOYMENT REASSESSMENT

On my deployment, I felt strong about living in my call. Just thinking about the fact that less than three years prior to us wrapping up the deployment I was in the middle of praying to figure out what was next for me, when I am confident all along that the uncertainty for me was in no way an uncertainty for God. He was in control of the situation because he was in charge of my destiny. It would not have been his destiny had I not been approved to serve as a chaplain.

I had received everything I sought out to pursue during the ten-month absence, mostly because there was a plan and a purpose. What I was not prepared for was the homecoming and all of the distractions that come with attempting to reintegrate, at that point, into a family of five.

All of a sudden, I was not a chaplain in Afghanistan but instead a husband and father of three young children, all of whom had significant expectations of me. The result was significant stress. The stress I had learned to manage in the deployment was much different than the stress that comes with negotiating children at home.

The extent of what I was experiencing was unlike anything I had experienced before. Sure, being a dad has its challenges. All of the attributes of impact that were identified earlier are what it takes to be the father that I want my children to have. But what I found was that chasing impact on the deployment and the successes that were found were actually adding an unreasonable amount of stress when it came to my family life.

Upon my arrival home, I wanted the ability to pursue the same personal goals, which came at a sacrifice to my family. Without recognizing it, I was compromising my family time for personal physical wellness aspirations.

This adrenaline high from deployment-related stress was resulting in some anger that I did not have a grasp on. I had no idea the extent of the stress really because living in it feels normal. Any conflict in the home between my two boys was a trigger. Any perceived threat of danger to anyone around me would also result in triggering unexplainable anger or rage. The protective posture I had established prior to the deployment had not ended but instead intensified. I wanted peace and safety, and I wanted it my way because I was the protector in my home. Peace and safety are two things not common in a family with young boys. Over the short term, I had lost the bearing of who I was supposed to be.

You might think that stress doesn't have anything to do with physical health, but in the conversation of thrive factors: stress, mental health, and emotional balance, directly relate to our body's ability to thrive physically and even to a larger extent spiritually, hence body, mind, and soul being three in one. I am not debating the science behind this, but instead attributing the value of being able to manage stress well, being mentally strong, and having emotional balance to thriving physically and spiritually.

It is not very often that people will associate physical health with mental health and certainly spiritual health, but they are not mutually exclusive. Stress of any magnitude is managed easier when the purpose in the given stress is identified and understood. Once I was able to recognize that my transition home resulted in a transition in responsibility and purpose, stress slowly began to reduce. The shifts of being in a perceivably controlled environment like Afghanistan to the uncontrolled environment of a chaotic home after a deployment helped me realize just how much mental health is a derivative of brain health and perspective, or spiritual health.

There continues to be tremendous value gained from the reintegration, part of which includes the importance of self-awareness and ability to thwart the onset of stress in the moment. In this, in conjunction with prayer, I have learned the value of the physiological action of deliberate breathing and its ability to lower the amped-up heart rate and help the brain escape the negative feedback loop through increased stress. It is hard to believe that something so easy like calculated and correct breathing can have such a tremendous effect on our body's ability to calm down. Knowing yourself well is a large part of determining what makes us thrive personally.

If my reintegration has taught me anything, it is the importance of knowing myself, what makes me thrive, and what things I am and am not willing to sacrifice in order to be well-rounded. This is of course for Christians relative to aligning with our faith and God's will for our lives.

I humbly admit that for the first time in my life, my capability to thrive physically is as high as it has ever been, mostly because of the success of the conditioning in my deployment, the recognition of previous issues, both positive and negative past experiences, and associating purpose to my health. I understand my body more now than ever and the ramifications of negotiating compensation to remain well.

If you were to ask me what my biggest takeaways from my experience in a physical fitness and wellness context would be, they are: goal management, transition of priorities, and the identification of what is and is not worth sacrificing. I believe this is something that anyone can relate to in various proportions, regardless of whether or not you have served in the military.

RECONCILIATION

What is the value here if you are not an individual who has served in the military? First and foremost, I believe it is about recognition of some of the issues that exist and encouraging individuals to be cognizant of how to mitigate them.

Physical wellness is such an integral part of our ability to live at our highest capacity, and for those who have deployed or served in the military, there are significant challenges associated with one or both. And I desire to help bring light to some of the issues that veterans face so we can get them on the road not only to recovery, but on the road to thriving and being influential. It is very difficult to be influential when we have not identified underlying issues contributing to not being at our best.

Upon my return, I went back in to do more biofeedback in order to help assess some of the health issues I had learned that are common after a deployment. These potential issues that may prevent someone from functioning optimally include: high levels of toxins in the system, unhealthy and excessive gut bacteria, increased inflammation, some sort of exposure to trauma, lung issues as a result of burn pits and toxic air, and adrenal fatigue as a result of prolonged stress.

This is not to say that everyone who serves in the military and deploys comes back with these issues. What I have learned in conversations with peer medical specialists, primarily in the natural and complementary health field, is that these are some of the issues that will affect a veteran's health, and the longer they are not addressed, the more formidable a challenge they can become.

Because I have experienced a variety of these issues personally, it is my recommendation that you or your loved one who has served in the military and perhaps in an overseas environment should schedule a visit with your local health provider that specializes in these issues for a comprehensive wellness exam.

This section on physical health and my experiences are not intended to serve as medical advice, but instead serve as sharing my personal experiences as they relate to my personal desire to thrive physically.

THRIVE FACTOR 3: FAMILY WELLNESS

"Behold, how good and pleasant it is when brothers dwell in unity!" (Psalm 133:1).

Out of the six thrive factors, family is the hardest for me to balance out and to thrive in. This is for a variety of reasons, some of which will be shared in this section, but most stem from the fact that I have found it is easiest for me to thrive when I am focused on the things I can control or are within my most immediate sphere of influence. I tend to neglect my family because the time it takes to instill family values and discipline is opportunity cost taken away from other things that have come easily. It is my natural inclination to resort to what I am proficient at, things outside this immediate sphere of influence.

Also because of this, I am a strong advocate in the fact that family wellness is an integral part of thriving. We can be thriving in all areas of our lives, yet if we have compromised our family for other pursuits or pleasures, we will not thrive and certainly be limited in our ability to live in impact. For some, family wellness takes significant work.

WAKE-UP CALL

One of the most difficult periods of my life started after coming back from Afghanistan in 2019. Reintegration from deployments is stressful for several reasons. I have already indicated some of the challenges I faced after my first deployment, so because of the first deployment's experiences, expecting hiccups in reintegration after a second deployment fifteen years later was reasonable. Despite having this expectation, the newness of the challenges made it complex.

The biggest difference in my 2004–2005 deployment from 2018–2019 is that I left three young children and a wife, which meant I had to reintegrate with my three young children and wife after they had learned to live without their dad and husband for that extended period. Naturally everyone had to readjust to accommodate the post-deployment dynamic; however, for my kids at three, five, and seven years old, it was hard to go back to an old normal. Thus you have the parents attempting to go back to the old normal of family responsibilities and intimacy while at the same time adjusting to a new normal with the children because they have little to no recollection of the old. I think with the arrival of our newest family member eleven months after I returned, it is safe to say which part of this equation was the easiest.

My honest opinion and certainly in my experience is that thriving in the family context is flat-out tough. My personal family construct is complicated, with two half-siblings on my mother's side and one half-sibling on my dad's side, all from marriages prior to my mom and dad being married. Then I have two stepsiblings from my mother's marriage after my dad. Among those half and stepsiblings are several nieces and nephews, some very close and others I have not seen in several years. Despite not being an only child, I was raised like an only child because of the vast age differences between my siblings and me.

Then on my wife's side of our family are her parents and two brothers. Between her two brothers, there are fifteen children total, bringing our three families to nineteen children. So in her family, the dynamics are much different, which have been a considerable part of my learning to adjust over the course of our marriage journey. Needless to say, our experiences growing up were vastly different, and we both had adjustments to make as we began our journey together.

It gets even more challenging when a family has miscarriages and an adoption that did not pan out as all had been anticipated. The reality of the situation is that these things occur more often than we realize, so our family dynamics are not much different from many families across our great land, but what may be different is how we respond and perceive these events and bumps in the road.

I keep going back to the reintegration process and experiences from 2019, likely because that is where there is value in our story and because I normally work with service members, veterans, and/ or their spouses. It serves the purpose of sharing with a broader audience.

Another reintegration story worth sharing is our tale of a post-deployment vacation that I took with my wife, children, and in-laws about a month after I returned from Afghanistan. The Christmas of 2018, our family was gifted a wonderful blessing of being able to visit Hawaii, specifically Maui, an island I had not been to in the Hawaiian Islands. Naturally I was excited, and my wife and kids were excited.

But our excitement was predicated on different components. I was excited because I had not had a chance to come down from prolonged exposure to stress and thought being on a beach would be relaxing, and my wife and kids were excited because we got to spend time together as a family and explore Maui. I anticipated relaxing without conditions; my family wanted conditional exploration. Go-go-go tends to be the nature of a family with young kids, and that was the energy on this particular vacation by all except yours truly. I was in complete recovery mode and wanted little to do with go-go-go.

While we were in Hawaii, which happened over my forty-first birthday, a wave of anxiousness came over me when my daughter expressed that she did not feel "loved on" enough. This prompted an immediate call to God for help. Her world was in chaos with my return, adjustment, and need for extra attention and love from me, and I flat-out was not living up to my obligation as a father. This was a wake-up call for me and an indication that my actions were not necessarily aligning with my words.

Hindsight is always 20/20, but my recognition of my personal ability to thrive, or live in impact, now is much different than it was even a year ago. It might be because I was in the beginning stages of adjusting from the deployment, but things certainly would be approached differently if we were to do the trip over again.

What I have come to realize since the trip is that in that situation, I compromised in my ability to support my family's ability to thrive. However, the compromise does not stem from me struggling during the trip because that was really outside my control due to coming out of the deployment and attempting to vacation with my family and in-laws so soon. Instead it comes from not knowing the optimal time to go on the trip. I simply had no idea at the time that when we choose the dates the timing would be poor, but the fact we did it so soon after my deployment could have been assessed better in order to protect my family and our ability to maximize the opportunity and vacation.

Gold Nugget: The other four thrive factors present incredible opportunity to live in impact for individuals, but there is room for compromise relative to an individual's prescription for thriving. Spiritual health and wellness and family wellness are no-compromise obligations. That is, if you are married and have a family, you cannot compromise in your steadfast pursuit of promoting the family's need and ability to thrive.

My last point is noteworthy simply because I have seen all too often husbands or wives who do not prioritize their relationship with each other or their responsibility to take a lead role in child development and character growth. More often than not, this does not end well, and as Stephen R. Covey is famous for saying, we want to "begin with the end in mind." Having a vision for the spiritual intimacy we should be pursuing in our relationship and family values and character of our children that we want to foster is imperative in the need to support our family's ability to thrive, both now and long term.

Not compromising my family's wellness is a point I am growing in. In my case, family wellness is the thrive factor most likely to keep me from thriving and living in impact, which means it is the one that will be the most intense to pursue and certainly the one that cannot be compromised in. This is an example of why it is important to embrace God's grace. Chasing impact has come at a cost at times to my family, and that is a drastic failure on my part as a result of misappropriated loyalty. The Lord knows that this is a work-in-progress for me.

When it comes to the six thrive factors and because our ability to thrive personally is dependent on others only in the family wellness context, loyalty becomes a contributing factor in our ability to thrive as a family, which is why I place the value on family wellness higher than the other nonspiritual wellness thrive factors. Even though my desire may be stronger to thrive physically, thriving physically means it will likely come at a cost to my family, or I am compromising family wellness for personal physical wellness, which again I would argue that there should not be compromise when it comes to family wellness. So my thrive factor of physical health looks different now than it did even a year and a half ago while I was deployed.

This remains true for career wellness, social wellness, and financial wellness as well. Essentially family wellness and our propensity to thrive is a by-product of our willingness to remain loyal to our family over being loyal to our career, recreational activities, peers, and even financial prosperity.

Since coming home from Maui, I have continued to find challenges relative to my deployment experience. Please don't get me wrong. My deployment experience was not anything close to what a lot of military chaplains experience; however, this does not take away the complexity that National Guard and Reserve soldiers have when dealing with reintegrating back into civilian life. This is why I was calling an active-duty chaplain recruiter as we were at the Maui airport getting ready to head home. I wanted to replicate what I had on the deployment, by continuing to serve a call and fill a void on active duty.

The one explanation I needed to hear was revealed in counseling shortly after I returned home, as it related to the challenges I was experiencing with my kids, is that the chaos and conflict in our home were not helping my desire to live in peace and protect my family. It is next to impossible at this stage we are in to live in peace. You could almost say it is like chasing impact without thriving. That attempt to promote peace in a home with three, now four, young children is next to impossible because of their nature to be in conflict.

I don't ever want to take my family for granted as they are the most important thing in my life outside of my relationship with God, but just like my relationship with God, I can compromise on my family for other less important things in my life. The one thing I will not compromise—and has been made very clear with my wife—is my desire to live up to my responsibility to provide for and protect our family, both spiritually and physically. I may not be perfect as a father, but my kids will always know that they and my wife are my priority because of the fact I won't compromise on taking care of them spiritually, financially, or physically.

Our immediate sphere of influence, which in this case is my family (those directly under my patriarchal leadership), should be the most important priority for living in impact. Unfortunately I had a gut check in the year prior to my deployment going through Dave Ramsey's Legacy Journey class. My gut check was that I was in fact compromising my family wellness for other purposes, including supporting others' welfare while my immediate family paid the price.

Opportunities we give in to that result in a compromise on our family's ability to thrive indicate our priorities in life, just like compromising on our spiritual disciplines and having time with God in morning devotion or going to church on Sundays show that a relationship with God is not a priority despite our words maybe indicating otherwise.

Because family can fall under a diverse and complicated construct, it is appropriate to break our responsibilities to each into three categories, by order of precedence: relationship with spouse, relationship with children, and relationship with other family members.

Despite being based on the order of precedence, I am going to change my approach to this dialogue by focusing on the most important last and starting with my responsibilities as a father.

RESPONSIBILITIES AS A PARENT

"Train up a child in the way he should go; even when he is old, he will not depart from it" (Proverbs 22:6 ESV).

When I think of family wellness, I think of the collective whole. I immediately think of the parent/children relationship along with the spiritual intimacy of the couple. For our sake here, I will only speak from my perspective and why it is vital for me as a dad to support my family's ability to thrive. For example, if my relationship with my children is suffering, then my relationship with my wife could very easily be out of balance. Or if my relationship with my wife is not optimal, it will likely affect my relationship with our kids (1 Timothy 5:8).

Let's face it. Being a parent in today's culture is challenging in and of itself. And when you add to it work responsibilities and extracurricular obligations that can get in the way, it can be easy to take a passive approach to parenting. I have found that our family's ability to thrive relative to my relationship with my children—or to be in unison—is predicated on three primary considerations: awareness, intention, and instruction.

If I am not thriving personally, then my energy is being mismanaged, but more often than not, it is because I am not aware or there is some peripheral stress interrupting my balance. My energy then gets utilized to get myself back in balance, which means I am neglecting something or someone else in my life. Typically it is my family.

So for my family to thrive, I must be thriving; thus my energy can also be utilized to help determine how to help my kids also thrive as individuals and collectively. This is perhaps the biggest reason that I still consider myself to be in a "chasing" mode.

The concepts of "character strengths" (Institute on Character) and "the five love languages" (Gary Chapman) are perfect examples of this in that if I am not aware of my own personal character strengths or love languages, it will be easy for me to have an empty tank without even knowing why it is the case. And the same is true for my kids. If I don't know what their character strengths or love languages are, there is no way I can support their effort to have a full tank or to be thriving. So not only do I need to be aware of my character strengths and love languages to support personal energy and ability to thrive, but I need to know my children's as well (and of course my wife's) and support their effort to align with them.

Both of these fundamental principles of energy management are only as valuable as our awareness of them.

1. Awareness: When it comes to awareness, not only is it vital for us to be cognizant of what our prescription to thrive looks like, but it also includes parents being cognizant of what that prescription looks like for our kids. Our three older children have vastly different prescriptions for their wellness as individuals, and then identifying how to leverage each of their individual thrive factors to help them thrive as a sibling team is imperative to family wellness.

2. Intention: Intention is where the rubber meets the road in this effort to be the best parents we can be. We know that everyone is busy, but how that busyness is managed will ultimately determine the trajectory, or path, that our kids take in life. Parenting takes intentional pursuit, and it takes us away from other things that we may place at a higher value than our children's character growth. But in all reality, there is not much more valuable in life than our direct influence and responsibility in character development and growth for our children.

   When we consider the value and importance of intention as it relates to our children's character growth, we have to look at it as an investment, one over time that will be exponentially more valuable than the value we place on their character growth at the time of influence.

   My intent to be transparent in this book in addressing my shortcomings is to bring light to the struggles that many of us have but do not get talked about. And parenting is certainly an area I fall short in, but it is an area I have a desire to grow in to help my children grow and develop into outstanding contributing members of the community they will live in someday. For me at the end of the day, it is my objective to be a better father to all of my children than I had growing up and for my boys to be better fathers when their time comes.

3. Instruction: Awareness and intention in parenting play important roles in helping children thrive, yet there is still a piece missing that needs to be addressed. Instruction plays the most integral part in this parenting equation. Instruction is predicated on the question of what I am teaching my children, not necessarily what others are teaching my children.

   I can reasonably assume that our societal approach to parenting, generally speaking, is that we allow others more opportunity to instruct our kids and shape their futures than we take the initiative in doing. But as a parent, it is our primary responsibility to instruct them on basic life principles that will help lead them to make sound decisions at the point they are led out into the real world. This certainly includes allowing them to fail and learn from their mistakes as minors, as the price paid for mistakes while someone is young is likely a lot cheaper than mistakes made later on down the road.

   As a Christian father, it is my obligation to teach them about God, right from wrong, humility, how to love, equality, US and world history, morality, grace, justice, work ethic, financial literacy, value of human life, importance of lifelong learning, health, and value of failure.

   To maximize our family's impact, we must create the framework to help our children recognize what that impact looks like. Being passive and not sharing our values with our children, not leveraging their strengths and promoting their ability to thrive individually and collectively, is a complete and utter failure on our part as parents.

   One of my biggest regrets now looking back on my adolescent years is that I was not concerned with maintaining vehicles, building projects, and even learning how to cook for myself. If there is any constructive advice that could be given to my teenage self, it would be to make sure to understand the importance of these basic responsibilities because someday there could very well be adolescent boys who will be looking to you for guidance on how to manage these things for themselves. And if you only know how to take a vehicle to a mechanic, are not comfortable building a tree house, or cannot make much more than a simple food dish, you are leaving a strong impression and not promoting basic life skills.

With all of this being said, it warrants me saying that I struggle mightily in parenting. I struggle mightily to find work/life balance. I even struggle at times in leveraging my children's character strengths and love languages for the good of our family. I struggle at putting aside the keyboard and picking up the fishing pole to do something with them that they enjoy doing, something that would be profitable for them. And I certainly struggle at managing the stress relative to being a father. But just like God's love for me, the one constant is that my love for my children doesn't change. It is my prayer that they will never question my love for them based on my love for Jesus and his love for us.

The role of parenting is represented not only with the children of the household, but also extends to caretaking (or serving) our parents as they age and are unable to take care of themselves. The biblical command of honoring our father and mother is not only a command, but it is also an offer of a promise, a promise of reward (Ephesians 6:2). Caretaking for our parents, as I have experienced, can place an extra burden on us, especially if we have children whom we are responsible for or if we feel that our parents fell short in their role in our upbringing. The command is not conditional, so despite our emotional attachment to our parents, we are obligated to serve our parents as they reach their later years and are unable to care for themselves.

Our role as parents on a much smaller scale parallels God's role in our lives. God has given us his Word to help us understand who he is and the expectations for us when we choose to follow his truth. We can fail. We can have success. But whether we give God the glory for the growth through the failure and the credit for the successes is up to us.

In the same way, we are to give biblical instruction and guide our children, letting them figure things out through failure and successes and trusting God with their paths and adherence to his call. The hard part about this is that this takes risk and compromise on our part, both of which are hard to absorb as parents. Just like the other resources that we will discuss later as part of God's economic system, our children are ours to nurture and manage as part of God's resources.

As I contemplate where we are in our family life cycle, amidst the fun and often trying times, I can only think about how fast time will fly by, and before we know it, we will be sending our last child out into the real world. My encouragement to myself, as well as to you, is to manage the opportunity to the best of your capabilities and let God lead. We don't want to look back and have regrets. Help those around you develop as a person and find their passions. Show them the value of discipline, hard work, serving others, and loving Jesus, and let them know that they are more important to you than your work but do not come before a relationship with God and your spouse.

RELATIONSHIP WITH OTHER FAMILY MEMBERS

Any married person can appreciate the fact that when we marry someone, we don't just end up in a relationship with that man or woman. We forge additional relationships with family members of the new spouse. Naturally the potential chaos with having in-laws is not as simple as just being able to neglect them, unlike our capability to manage toxic relationships in our own family.

We must recognize people for what and who they are and manage any chaos that comes from these relationships by limiting the ability for a toxic relationship to influence our ability to thrive as an individual and family.

This is not to say that our in-law relationships will all be chaotic or, to another extent, toxic, but for a marriage and family to thrive, there needs to be continuity with in-laws (especially parents); and an ideal way to establish continuity is to be fully transparent in the desired direction that the family is pursuing in order to manage expectations.

While we get to choose our spouse and friends we spend ample time with, we are not as fortunate to be able to choose our own family members or in-laws. Thus, nurturing relationships with our own family and in-laws by loving them unconditionally, managing the chaos, and investing in the relationships that help support the family are productive ways to help us in our goal of thriving as a family.

SPIRITUAL MARITAL INTIMACY

> Intimacy is ...
> a Focus on Spiritual Growth and Oneness;
> a Journey, not a Destination;
> a Relationship that Bears all Burdens;
> a Craving from the Soul;
> Fervent Prayerful Support;
> Passionate Love;
> Christ Centric;
> and Blending of Two Hearts. (Personal Reflection on Spiritual Intimacy)

All husbands and Christian men should pay close attention to this part of the book. I will even keep it short and to the point. Our role as a father has already been expressed, and it is important, but if we neglect our role as a husband, we fail to live up to our responsibility as a Christian man leading our household. And just like being a father, we don't want to wake up down the road with regrets in the most important relationship we will ever have on this earth next to our relationship with Jesus.

I can remember a conversation with my wife shortly after we started dating that was prompted by her inquiry of what I envisioned for marriage. My answer was that I wanted to wake up at eighty years old with no regrets and more in love with my wife at that point than any other point in our marriage. And when I think of the couples who model spiritual intimacy, I don't think of a perfect marriage (because it doesn't exist). I specifically think of their spiritual growth as a couple, their profound spiritual connection, and their unconditional love that has helped them stand the test of time.

While I have many models of couples for what an ideal marriage looks like, my in-laws are as close to a perfect example of what a spiritual intimate marriage looks like and what I hope our relationship emulates twenty-five years from now. Even after over forty-five years of being married, they exhibit all of the facets of spiritual intimacy that I shared at the beginning of this section. In fact, it can even still get a little awkward. The idea of spiritual intimacy in a marriage may be a concept that is foreign to those even within the church.

Gold Nugget: Spiritual intimacy is the notion that a relationship between a husband and a wife is centered on their relationship with God, and the more spiritually mature the couple grows, the more spiritually mature the marriage becomes. In other words, God serves as the guidepost throughout the relationship. It is a marriage grounded in a covenantal promise with God and not just a marriage confirmed by a license from a state. Spiritual intimacy should be the target for Christian marriage, and it begins and ends with God.

Spiritual intimacy is echelons beyond the sexual intimacy and relationship between a man and woman, although we can never discount the vitality of a sexually strong marriage. It is the idea that a man and woman become one (Mark 10:6–9) and that there is nothing that can break the bond with each other because the marriage and reliance on God is greater than the sum of its parts. The relationship with God increases the capacity and capabilities that drive the journey, and the relationship between the husband and wife is met with the same attributes and spiritual fruit that come from the Holy Spirit. Spiritual intimacy is sacrificial and unconditional, meaning both individuals put their spouse above their own self and do not set conditions in any facet of their relationship.

We simply cannot offer love, grace, gratitude, security, hope, and equity to our spouse without understanding these notions through a biblical lens and the offer that God gave to us through Jesus. To the world, these words have different meanings and often get defined relative to cultural tendencies; however, biblically defined, they have truth and are absolute, with no variation or fluidity. What God proclaimed in his Word stood firm when it was scribed. It stands firm now, and it will stand firm until Jesus returns.

As I have already pointed out, the ideas of awareness and intention are keen in parenting, but they are even more important in the concept of spiritual intimacy. In order for a marriage to thrive, the needs of the spouse have to be put above the needs of self, but one can only put the needs of their spouse ahead of their own if they are aware of those specific needs.

Gary Chapman in his classic book *The Five Love Languages* has identified the five love languages as physical touch, words of affirmation, quality time, acts of service, and gift-giving. Awareness of a spouse's love language without intention of filling the spouse's love tank will significantly limit the spiritual intimacy and ability to thrive as a couple.

Christian men, in addition to what I have stated previously, you have two ideals that cannot be compromised on relative to your role as a husband.

1. You must put your spouse ahead of every other relationship (excluding your relationship with Jesus) in your life, including your children, and personal thrive factors. We will never thrive personally if we are not thriving in our marriages.
2. It is your responsibility to chart your family's course and lead the way based on shared family values, beliefs, and prayer. If you do not have a path to lead your wife, regardless of your intention, your ability to live in impact as a family will never be aligned with your capability to live in impact.

Just like my desire to grow in love with my wife shared in the mentioned conversation prior to being married, despite the foreseen and unforeseen challenges, we are growing as a couple daily. We also offer each other unconditional grace, and our marriage stands firm on the rock that is Christ. It is hard to tell where our marriage would be without Jesus, and I certainly do not know where I would be without Jesus as my cornerstone. In order for our Christian marriages to endure, we cannot compromise on our submission to each other and God as the light for our path.

Part of my daily prayer is to endure the challenges, struggles, and chaos I face as a man, husband, and father. Without God's grace, endurance would be impossible.

FAMILY UNITY

"As for me and my house, we will serve the Lord" (Joshua 24:15).

Part of the nature of having a young and growing family is that there is always chaos. Our family lives in chaos. But what having a young and growing family does not mean is that in the midst of chaos, unity cannot be lived in. For me, there is nothing more powerful than having unity in our home. This has not been the norm, but when there has been unity, as a family we thrive. I guess you could say we thrive in the face of unity and with the potential to thrive also in the face of adversity when we are united as a family.

If the recipe to thrive as a family includes some sort of unity, then there needs to be a method to manage the chaos that is brought on by the demands of the world. The only way to manage the chaos is to prayerfully have a plan, or a charted course, to travel down when the chaos occurs. Just like in battle, without prayer, a plan, and armor, the chaos simply gets more intense, and the likelihood to be victorious lessens.

Your question may then be in addition to prayer, what the plan, or charted course, to manage chaos should look like. There are four biblical no-compromise suggestions that I would like to highlight to assist in this effort.

1. Parents must be in control of the environment (Ephesians 6:1–3).
2. Family values must be identified and exhibited/taught by parents (Ephesians 6:1–3).
3. Parents must prioritize time alone together (Ephesians 5:25–28).
4. Everyone makes compromise for the good of the family (James 1:22–25).

All of these suggestions are essentially self-explanatory, so I will refrain from elaborating on each of them. But for our purpose, it is important to note that I am listing them because they are foundational principles that will help a family thrive. Foundational principles indicate that they are principles that cannot be compromised on. No-compromise principles include managing immediate family chaos and not neglecting immediate family because of the chaos.

Before we move on though, I do want to take special note of the second suggestion of family values needing to be identified, exhibited/taught by parents, and visible for the family to reflect on regularly. I cannot stress the importance of this enough in that the family's ability to thrive and propensity for communal impact will be limited without, at the very least, a family mission statement.

For additional ideas to extend on this concept of establishing family unity, I strongly encourage you to look into resources like Dave Ramsey's Legacy Journey Training Course or Stephen Covey's *7 Habits to a Highly Successful Family.*

Developing a family mission statement takes significant reflection and prayer, and once developed, it serves as the compass to get the family headed in the right direction. The Legacy Journey expands on this development by helping identify a family's purpose statement, priorities, value system, goals and dreams, skills and abilities, and core values. Other free resources and tools accessible online promote these techniques to help develop family wellness.

Before my previous deployment, my wife and I took a short trip by ourselves and focused on these exact details to help us navigate through the chaos of the deployment that was about to come. As a husband and father, this has likely been the most profitable contribution I have made to support my family's ability to thrive and eventually live in impact.

If I were to deploy again, I would take the same approach to reaffirm our commitment to each other and establish goals to help us have a targeted approach throughout the deployment, which at the end of the deployment affords the opportunity to celebrate victories as a family. It is important to celebrate victories when we are in the chaos of deployment and life in general.

THRIVE FACTOR 4: CAREER WELLNESS

"Whoever works his land will have plenty of bread, but he who follows worthless pursuits lacks sense" (Proverbs 12:11).

When my wife and I were dating and I met her dad for the first time, I remember a conversation that I will never forget. He asked me what I wanted to do for a living, essentially when I grew up. At the time, it was apparent that I was searching for purpose and meaning, and to his credit, he knew I was spiritually immature. Little did I know he was assessing how connected to my purpose I was at the time.

I recall hesitating and thinking, *Well, my dad owned a health club, and I thought that was cool.* So my response to him was that I wanted to be in the fitness industry. Really what was on my heart at the time was to own a facility that would allow high school athletes to train year-round indoors in Montana.

What I also remember about this first visit with her parents was that after they left, Angie informed me that she had had a conversation with her dad where he expressed disappointment. Like any dad with one daughter who wants the best for her, he had higher hopes for whom she would end up meeting, eventually falling in love with, and marrying. I was not who Angie's dad had expected her to spend the rest of her life with. And now as a dad of two daughters myself, I can empathize with my father-in-law.

What I did not know at the time was how exactly to answer Angie's dad's question. Perhaps it was because I was incredibly nervous or I had just recently returned from Iraq going through some work-related challenges. Purpose was the last thing on my mind. Regardless of what it was, I was unaware that what I was going to do for a living needed to directly coincide with purpose.

The question posed from my father-in-law was the first time in my life that I was challenged to start attaching purpose to career. Not only did it challenge me, but it also prompted motivation, otherwise it would not have resonated with me the way it does fifteen years later.

FAITH-CENTERED LIVING

"Now the eleven disciples went to Galilee, to the mountain to which Jesus had directed them. And when they saw him, they worshiped him, but some doubted. And Jesus came and said to them, 'All authority in heaven and on earth has been given to me. Go therefore and make disciples of all nations, baptizing them in the name of the Father and of the Son and of the Holy Spirit, teaching them to observe all that I have commanded you. And behold, I am with you always, to the end of the age.'" (Matthew 28:16–20)

If we consider these words of Jesus in Matthew, we have to consider how they directly relate to our lives and the notion that we are to live out this command in its entirety, all the time, and not separating ministry from other aspects of our lives. This is at the core derived from perspective and our soul purpose. We are to live entirely as disciples of Jesus and for Jesus always, not selectively choose when we live out our faith in different aspects of our lives.

When it comes to career wellness, five areas should be heavily considered for one to thrive and essentially live in impact. These areas are not relative to our salvation but are relative to purpose and aligning our faith with how we make a living. Despite what we do vocationally, we are called to follow Jesus and glorify him through our work, and we can do that in various capacities. These areas are vocation, service/volunteering, lifelong learning/education, extracurricular hobbies, and being able to understand current events.

These five facets of career/vocational wellness correlate biblically, and the reason I have placed them under this category is because they all have the significant ability to promote thriving and especially impact when they are conducted in accordance with scripture.

This is not a conversation about having to do these things as a Christian, as Jesus and the writers in the New Testament are clear about faith being a heart issue. Instead this is a matter of the heart and our actions responding to God's call in our lives. We will touch briefly on each facet to give a better idea of their importance in the conversation as they relate to thriving and impact.

VOCATION (FOR COMPENSATION AND WITHOUT)

"Whatever you do, work heartily, as for the Lord and not for men, knowing that from the Lord you will receive the inheritance as your reward. You are serving the Lord Christ" (Colossians 3:23).

I can thank my father-in-law for this, but one of my favorite conversations to have with individuals is about their work, or what they do to make a living. There is so much opportunity in this to discuss spiritual health without them being aware of our conversation being about their spiritual health. This is the area where I really get to learn more about an individual's values, beliefs, skills, and how they interpret being able to contribute to something bigger than themselves. Unfortunately, not everyone sees this type of opportunity through assessing career wellness.

Even for us as Christians, we can get away from this notion that what we do for a living is an extension of our faith. It just is. We want to make sure that we are aligning our knowledge, skills, abilities, gifts, values, and interests with the primary motivational factor of being the hands and feet of Jesus, no matter what our occupation is, or how we are spending our time.

Every aspect of impact as we defined previously is relevant here. And when we are working in our soul purpose, it does not feel like work; nor does it matter who we work for because living in purpose vocationally is more important to our ability to thrive than what we actually do.

If we are connected to our soul purpose vocationally, just like generally in life, we are more inclined to navigate through the challenges associated with the mundane aspects of work successfully because we are soul-focused on the purpose instead of the mundane.

In my experience, two primary considerations will affect our ability to focus on the purpose instead of the ordinary.

1. We want to make sure our values align with the organization that we spend a majority of our time with. Value alignment will not only help us keep the focus, but it also helps the organization or business create the culture that they are actively attempting to generate. And if we are in a leadership position in the organization or business, we want to make sure that we have defined and articulated our values and the team members being added fit in our values set as well.

Contrarily, if an organization or business is not up-front about their values or mission, there will likely be a significant disconnect, meaning the challenges and mundane aspects will be stronger than the ability to focus on fulfilling our soul purpose.

Additionally, if the organization or business does not indicate or express their values, it is also highly likely that they will not be concerned with the ability of their team to live out their values, which ends up being a losing proposition for both parties.

2. Next is really an extension of the first consideration. How will this career affect the work/life balance? Is it work/life balance friendly? Or will the work reduce the margin needed to be able to pursue the larger scope of impact?

The reality of the situation is that impact generated is not just about one facet of our lives. Impact is about being able to be influential in the home; it is about being influential in the office or whatever the work environment looks like. It is also about being influential in the community. It is about the pursuit of a macrolevel vision. The impact in the home, work, and community would all be considered independent, microlevel pursuits, which obviously serves their purposes, but we are talking bigger. We are talking macrolevel, extraordinary, and life-changing impact.

If we don't have the margin to be influential in other areas, then we miss out on the intent. But as has been discussed, this looks different for everyone and is exactly why the thrive action plan includes all of the thrive factors and being able to develop an all-encompassing prescription.

Whether one is a real estate agent, military officer, landlord, or CEO of a Fortune 500 company, it is not the occupation that matters. It is the opportunity presented and the connection one has with their soul purpose. That is what matters in order to thrive.

SERVICE/VOLUNTEERING

"Then he said to his disciples, 'The harvest is plentiful, but the laborers are few; therefore, pray earnestly to the Lord of the harvest to send out laborers into his harvest'" (Matthew 9:37).

Serving as a Christian or Christian family is as innate as it can get. The more we mature in Christ, the more we become like him. When we see a spiritually healthy Christian or Christian family, it is often indicative of their heart to serve. Serving is a spiritual discipline in which we must match our faith with our actions (Galatians 6:6–10).

Whether one is serving in a local church or for a local food pantry, nonprofit organization, or global missions organization, the point is not where but why. And just like our entire dialogue promoting soul purpose, the why of serving others is to be the hands and feet of Jesus or to live as Jesus lived with a heart to serve so others recognize God is at work. There can be no other primarily faith-based motivation to serve others.

We do not have to actually wash others' feet like Jesus did in the upper room, but we should have the willingness and heart to humble ourselves when called to do so. This could be metaphorically or out of necessity. In service, the point is to be willing and able to do what the Holy Spirit prompts us to do.

Similar to vocation, we want to make sure that we are aligning our knowledge, skills, abilities, spiritual gifts, values, and interests with the primary motivational factor of being the hands and feet of Jesus. If we are not doing things we enjoy while we serve others, the endurance to persevere through some of the challenges that come with serving will be minimized.

On the other hand, when we invest in things we love doing and have passion for, like mentoring youth, hunting, raising and caring for animals, or exploring the great outdoors in general, then there is an opportunity to be of service with an abundance of organizations. The sky really is the limit, and there is undoubtedly a need for strong discipleship everywhere you look.

Just like following Jesus, the call to serve is an act of obedience on our part that is solidified through prayer. The call to serve could be in the military. It could be as a pastor, medical missionary, or, as in my case, a founder of a nonprofit organization. Service, in this context, usually means that you will personally be giving up something of value (personal resources such as time or finances) to benefit others.

I can humbly admit that before I had stepped into faith and a relationship with Jesus in late 2005, serving would have been the last thing on my to-do list and mind. Even my reason for joining the Montana Army National Guard was out of selfishness. The fact that it would pay for my education and hopefully square me away and get me on a different path than the one I was heading down was my primary motivation.

After all, I had the luxury of seeing what the United States Navy did for my brother, changing his path in life exponentially, and even though I had visited with air force, navy, and Army National Guard recruiters, the ability to stay in Montana while getting the benefits of being in the military proved to be the best option for me, selfishly. Because we were pre-9/11, there was no threat globally, which meant my time in the Army National Guard would allow me to support our state in natural disasters and state emergencies.

Twenty-one years later, I can say, "But God ..." The difference between my heart to serve in the military when I joined and the service I am invested in now is that everything done today is through the lens of faith and prayerfully considered, which makes it that much more meaningful and, you guessed it, impactful.

LIFELONG LEARNING/EDUCATION

"For this very reason, make every effort to add to your faith goodness; and to goodness, knowledge; and to knowledge, self-control; and to self-control, perseverance; and to perseverance, godliness; and to godliness, mutual affection; and to mutual affection, love" (2 Peter 1:5–7).

Peter's second letter to the churches of Asia Minor was a warning to them to stay in tune with the teachings of God, growing in knowledge through his Word. I believe this warning holds as true now as it has at any point in history. The only way we can pursue spiritual maturity, as Peter encouraged, is through an intimate connection with God's Word. It is clear and simple. Our spiritual growth is directly related to our relationship with the God of the Bible, not anything else.

A man's character and reflection of his heart are defined by what is on his bookshelf or, perhaps now, what is playing on the podcast app. Just like finances, with time being a resource that we are managing for God, we have a responsibility to manage it well. Unfortunately this is not something that has been valued to the point that time aligns with the pursuit of spiritual growth. Naturally what occurs is spiritual lethargy. Books to promote spiritual growth don't get opened, hearts and minds become stagnant, and God simply becomes an afterthought or is put in a box that is convenient for one's faith.

As we have discussed, faith is not about our definition of what it needs to look like. Faith is about recognizing that the God of the universe has a plan for us, a soul purpose, and understanding that we have to pursue him. We have to pursue understanding his character. In turn, we glean wisdom from his Word, and he communicates with us through the intimate connection that comes with reading the Bible. We do not grow spiritually without this connection. And we cannot spiritually thrive and live influentially without the connection.

This engagement, this understanding of who God is, comes from the faith-based lens generated through this relationship. The perspective will generate a passion in your heart that is so intense that pursuit of everything becomes purposeful. Pursuit of social justices shifts according to scriptural values and the understanding of God's plan for humanity. It changes the perspective on abortion, equality, and sexual immorality.

As Christians, we are not called to take a seat in the back row but instead to speak out for these moral injustices. Someday we will have to answer for our response to these issues and being passive or not aligning with the biblical moral code is certainly not a place I want to be positioned. Thus, we must grow in the Word to be able to position us better for this spiritual warfare battle.

EXTRACURRICULAR ACTIVITIES

"There is nothing better for a person than that he should eat and drink and find enjoyment in his toil. This also, I saw, is from the hand of God" (Ecclesiastes 2:24).

Growing up, all I knew was sports. We can blame that one on my dad. We ate, drank, and slept sports when I was with him. Ever since I can remember, I was in the stands of the old University of Montana football stadium watching the Grizzlies play their Big Sky Conference football rivals. This was back in the day before they were perennial conference champions.

Between my favorite sport to play, baseball, and with football and basketball in the mix, I don't think I could reasonably count the number of hours or time that was put into playing a game of some sort. We would play basketball until midnight in the summers, oftentimes until a neighbor yelled at us to stop making so much noise. Those were certainly the good ole days.

Unfortunately for me, sports became an obsession, or an addiction, that when I wasn't playing it was on the television. That was all that was on my television. It was an obsession until I started to realize that life certainly had more to offer than thinking sports were relevant, or purposeful, in my life. That perspective shift and seeing things differently made me realize that there were better ways to spend my time.

I have gone as far as calculating how many hours can be invested into watching football, or any sport for that matter, during any given season. Honestly, it is appalling, especially considering that we can be subjected to many seasons of spectating and truly wasting precious time.

Here is the reason I bring this to light. If we are talking energy management, creating margin to invest in the most important things in our lives, and living in soul purpose, then spending thousands of hours in any given year watching sports that we do not have any direct connection to is not something that fits these parameters.

If we are talking about working with kids or young adults, teaching them a game and mentoring them to be better stewards and ambassadors for Jesus on the playing field, then this is a different conversation. I know I could have used this type of mentorship in my life growing up.

This is just my example of time spent in personal extracurricular activities not being fruitful. But really it can be translated to just about anything that has reduced value due to the disconnect from purpose. We have an obligation as Christians to do everything with purpose and intent, which means maximizing opportunities even in the extracurricular things we love to do, above and beyond what we do for a living and in service.

My new personal extracurricular enjoyment that I will discuss in greater detail later is in music. And even though I had the blessing of being able to travel to Europe with a Montana-based boys' choir as a ten-year-old, I was not gifted with musical talent. This does not deter my interest, specifically my personal investment in music-related extracurricular activities.

My wife and I thoroughly enjoy traveling regionally to see our favorite band, Needtobreathe. This is our escape, our marital getaway as often as we can arrange it, but it is even more than that. Music, whether it is Needtobreathe, Switchfoot, Lauren Daigle, Sanctus Real, or any of our other favorite bands, are energy-producers. There is just something about good music that charges us.

Unlike my musically gifted wife, I have found my investment in music, my connection to how I can give glory to God, by utilizing my spiritual gifts and love for music in other ways down the road.

AWARENESS OF CURRENT AFFAIRS

"But grow in the grace and knowledge of our Lord and Savior Jesus Christ. To him be the glory both now and to the day of eternity. Amen" (2 Peter 3:18).

It is my personal evaluation that the church is a mixed bag when it comes to its ability to manage current affairs. It is not in my interest here to evaluate the church in this regard, but instead to exhort the church to pay attention to and prayerfully manage our role as Christians and faithfully represent Jesus Christ in how we navigate through the challenges associated with what is going on in our culture.

The secular world is paying close attention to how Christians respond to the cultural issues of our day, and it is up to us to manage them with abundant love and grace, knowing that Jesus is on full display through our words and actions. Unfortunately individuals both inside and outside the church are paying attention and basing their interpretation of who Jesus is by how we act. We cannot apply emotions to this, but to simply recognize it for what it is and in order for us to fulfill the responsibility of making disciples, we are to represent Jesus well.

Whether it is politics, broadcast journalism, global affairs, or day-to-day trends, we are to respond in the same manner that we would in any other area that we have visited in this section on career wellness. We are Christians living in a secular world, of which we have no control over, but what we do have is influence over how we communicate in both word and deed the moral construct that we are to align with. This is another area that there is no compromise in, as God has made it very clear that there is a distinct separation between what the world says is OK and what he deems immoral conduct. It is vital that we are on the side of God being our moral authority and the Bible as the source for absolute truth.

Ultimately, thriving in a career/vocational context means one is soul-motivated to utilize their God-given knowledge, skills, abilities, and gifts. It can be difficult to thrive and be influential without having this soul motivation and pursuit to live in purpose primarily because of the transition and pivot points that offer opportunity to get perceivably taken off one's path. Someone may be heading in the direction that God has called them in, yet when life happens and transitions occur without eyes fixed on Jesus, the course can easily get diverted.

TRANSITION AND PIVOT POINTS

Life has a funny way of projecting us on different paths than perhaps we expect to be going down. The important thing to understand as Christians is that we are not the author of our own story and that if we are on a path that we trust God is leading us down and a transition or pivot occurs, we have to remain steadfast in that faith and trust to recognize it is all a part of the journey. This is especially hard to do if we are spiritually young and new to this journey of faith.

We have more influence in our transitions because they can be seen prior to reaching them. Transitions are life's planned events. Pivot points are not necessarily life's planned events yet are inevitable in the journey, which makes our spiritual health a vital component in being able to trust God through these pivotal moments.

Transitions can include points that we make important decisions, major life events (like graduations, weddings, planned career change, military deployment, location changes, and loss), and pivot points would include trauma-related events or events that we don't have an opportunity to pray and plan for. They just occur as a part of life.

Transitions and pivot points in life can be extremely difficult to endure when the perspective or focus is on the event itself instead of the purpose one is being brought through. If we detach from the purpose of why God brings us through challenges, we miss out on the value of the event itself. Our spiritual health provides endurance, or our hope, faith, and identity, all the attributes of our spiritual health, help lead and guide us through transitions and pivot points.

Think about it this way. If our identity is tied to our career, there will be a crisis when retirement occurs. When we have no hope, we will suffer mightily in grief with the loss of someone close. And without faith, there will be tremendous challenges associated with any event in life that is difficult to navigate through. God did not give us a spirit of fear, so living without the protection of the Holy Spirit is detrimental to our spiritual health and ability to face transition and pivot points (2 Timothy 1:7).

NEVER A WASTED OPPORTUNITY

When I think of career wellness, I think specifically of leveraging and maximizing one's knowledge, skills, and abilities by aligning them with interests that are going to allow others to be blessed.

I think of businesses like Chick-Fil-A, Dave Ramsey's Lampo Group, and Hobby Lobby. The individuals who are putting themselves in positions to succeed vocationally by working for one of these entities, whether entry-level or in management, are not only going to thrive personally, but they are going to naturally live in an environment that breeds impact in their community. These are just three examples out of thousands of Christian companies that offer this same type of spiritual value as an employee.

Spiritual wellness and one's strong desire to not waste their knowledge, skills, and abilities by not aligning what they bring to the table with, values and interests will maximize the opportunities. And no matter what the current knowledge, skills, and ability are, there is opportunity to increase future capacity just with a desire to grow in these areas.

It may be hard to comprehend, but the contribution made goes well beyond the vocation itself. The contribution, or impact, is found in the opportunity to serve instead of receive and gain value and experience over simply performing a function or filling a responsibility. There is always more to gain than what meets the eye.

At the end of the workday, we want to be in a position that we know we are contributing to something much greater than ourselves, and when our time in the workforce is done or our margin for volunteering is increased, we also want to know that we are fulfilling our responsibility to give honor to God through our work.

THRIVE FACTOR 5: SOCIAL HEALTH

"I am not bound to win, but I am bound to be true. I am not bound to succeed, but I am bound to live by the light that I have. I must stand with anybody that stands right, and stand with him while he is right, and part with him when he goes wrong" (Abraham Lincoln).

Just like the spiritual intimacy that we talked about previously that should exist in a marriage, there is a soulful connection with Christian peers that is available for Christians to pursue. That is not to say, however, that all friendships will offer that soul tie that binds two people eternally through Christ. The soulful connections are dependent on both individuals being proximally close to God.

An example of this soulful connection is David (shepherd boy turned warrior) and Jonathan (prince and son of King Saul) as found in the Old Testament. Despite fearing for his life, David was honest with Jonathan and shared the fact that he felt his life was in jeopardy and that Jonathan's dad, Saul, the king of Israel, wanted to kill him. The trust and priority of relationships with God and each other is what ultimately saved David from being killed by

King Saul. Jonathan did not betray David but instead allowed him to escape the planned execution.

If you read 1 Samuel 20, you will find the details of this soul connection. Details emerge of David paying homage to Jonathan by bowing three times in utmost respect, the two of them exchanging kisses (as a custom of the culture) and then weeping together. In verse 42, their godly connection is validated when Jonathan says to David, "Go in peace, for we have sworn friendship with each other in the name of the Lord, saying, 'The Lord is witness between you and me, and between your descendants and my descendants forever.'"

Common threads in any strong relationship (not limited to soulful connections) are trust, being able to be vulnerable, and transparency without conditions. Strong relationships will not be forged without these three threads. In any relationship, if trust, vulnerability, and transparency are evident, the likelihood that the relationship will prosper is significant, leading to healthy connections.

HEALTHY CONNECTIONS

"A man of many companions may come to ruin, but there is a friend who sticks closer than a brother" (Proverbs 18:24).

I would like you to consider something for a minute. Considering your strengths and weaknesses, would you be better or worse off being surrounded by five individuals exactly like you? Now consider being surrounded by a strong, diverse group of people who complement your strengths and weaknesses and whether you would be better or worse off.

When we consider social wellness and our ability to thrive as a result of it, several factors come into play. Social wellness includes being engaged with people sharing common interests but also having the ability to have healthy relationships with those you do not align thinking with. This could be religious thinking, political thinking, or just having generally different viewpoints. Social wellness and healthy connections also include managing expectations of others and understanding personal biases relative to how they affect our relationships with others.

Whether we recognize it or not, individuals around us influence our ability to thrive. This could be those we have connections with through church, work, play, or the neighborhoods in which we live.

Our ability to thrive socially includes having honest and constructive criticism/dialogue with those of opposing views or beliefs. It is my experience that we are actually better off surrounding ourselves with people who offer complementary value and who we can engage open and honest dialogue with than if we are only surrounding ourselves with those of like-mindedness but offering minimal constructive dialogue. The key is the ability to have open and honest dialogue without being destructive.

> *Gold Nugget: The value gained in a healthy connection is derived more from the ability to have constructive and honest dialogue than it is strictly by sharing common interests.*

There is a place for value gained from common interests in this context of thriving socially; however, we will postpone this part of the conversation for the time being.

As church, work, play, or our neighbors have been mentioned as being an integral part of our social connections, it is necessary to pay attention to the toxicity that can be found in relationships. One of the biggest and most difficult lessons I have learned in life is to avoid the wolves disguised as sheep. They will be in your circle of influence, and it will be difficult to identify and rid yourself of them, but you will be better off for it.

Toxic relationships are what I would deem to be one of the

more influential factors when it comes to limiting the ability to thrive socially, and as discussed previously, we all have the need to manage the chaos or toxic relationships in our lives, whether they are through our family or other connections.

Managing social chaos and toxic relationships have more to do with our own spiritual health and wellness than it does attempting to manage others. As we already addressed, it is not feasible to attempt to manage other perspectives, just as it is not possible to attempt to manage others' actions. What we can influence is how we manage the expectations of others and our own personal biases. Both of these tenets are paramount in the pursuit of promoting healthy connections.

EXPECTATION MANAGEMENT

When I think about expectation management in the context of relationships, I think specifically about what Jesus says in John 2:23–25, "Now when he was in Jerusalem at the Passover Feast, many believed in his name when they saw the signs that he was doing. But Jesus on his part did not entrust himself to them, because he knew all people and needed no one to bear witness about man, for he himself knew what was in man."

Can you imagine the results of our relationships if we approached them in this manner, if we limited our expectations of others because we already know that others (as well as ourselves) are imperfect beings in need of extensive grace? In essence, the lens through which we see others directly influences how we approach our relationships, not only with those we are naturally supposed to have strong relationships with but also those who look, think, and act differently than we do. Mismanaging our relationships according to how others, simply stated, look, think, and act are what are commonly known as biases, which can be positive or negative based on one's perception of the world.

UNDERSTANDING BIASES

Biases are real. I have them. You have them, both hidden and unhidden. One's family makeup, skin color, residence, profession, education level, belief system, parental treatment, and so forth all create hidden and unhidden biases. Biases themselves are amoral. They are only as destructive as one's perception of the world. Biases can also be constructive, meaning they can be productive, primarily when they are unhidden. Biases can promote your desire to work with someone of different persuasion to forge progress moving forward for mutual benefit.

Biases become destructive when one gets stuck thinking their situation is better than someone else's or when they only work with people with the same biases to address their perceived problem. Biases can lead to prejudices and racism, but that is not always the case.

The problem is not the bias itself. The problem is instead perspective, the lens through which one sees the world, or their worldview. The perspective, or worldview, drives agenda and ultimately gets a group of people working toward their agenda or common bias. This can create immense negative energy and be consuming and certainly counterproductive.

It comes down to perspective aligning with good or evil, and unfortunately we don't always recognize which side we are on. This is why spiritual health and worldview are so vital to assess regularly. What we may think is part of our soul purpose may actually align with evil. This is known as disillusionment. To avoid getting too deep theologically, disillusionment is simply the notion that things are not as they appear. A veil is keeping someone or multiple people from being able to see the situation for what it is instead of what is perceived.

It is one's heart abiding with what God has done for us that will align us with his goodness and save us from our sin. God has a bias for us, as part of his creation, and holds no prejudices toward anyone. We are all the same in his eyes; therefore we should see others the same in ours if we live by confessing with our mouth and believing with our heart that Jesus is Lord (Romans 10:9). Recognizing things as they are as Jesus did and not as they appear is this spiritual discipline of disillusionment and vital in understanding and managing biases.

If they are causing tension or destruction in your relationships, then there is a need to consider and perhaps start shifting your worldview. Open up a Bible to the book of Ephesians or James, and read about how our sin nature, Satan, and the world have a grasp on us until our heart and perspective are fixed on Jesus. Most of all, it is important to assess whether biases are interfering with spiritual health and wellness and the ability to thrive because of emotional instability. Prayer will certainly assist in this determination.

Because impact is ultimately about others, it can strongly be suggested that how we treat others outside our comfort zones, or our own personal biases, influences our capacity for impact.

MENTORSHIP IS INVESTMENT

When I think about one's ability to thrive in the thrive factors, I think about the importance of growth and the concept of mentorship. It is not optimal to think that a person should only have one mentor, but instead a mentor for every area that is relative to thriving.

For example, if I am struggling in my faith journey or my role as a husband or father, my responsibility is to find the means to be able to grow in my faith or as a dad, essentially to promote my ability to thrive. The same is true for my role as a chaplain or perhaps as an organizational leader. But the mentor who may be ideal for growing in my faith may not be the optimal mentor for physical health and wellness.

Mentorship, from my perspective, is one of the most important factors for pursuing impact and the ability to thrive. Our ability to be the best version of ourselves is largely based on our ability to surround ourselves with the people who promote high functioning.

You will find this throughout the Bible, but the relationship I think of immediately is the apostle Paul's work with Timothy and equipping him for ministry.

My personal journey as the organizational leader for Impact Montana has been a blessing in large part because of the opportunities I have had to serve as a mentor and the ability to walk alongside some veterans who have faced tremendous battles outside their military service.

One story I cannot help but share is without a doubt a narrative that is a result of God's handiwork. I had a new neighbor whom I knew was a Marine, but because of various reasons unknown to me at the time, he had not interacted with me for at least five months after his family had moved in. All I knew was that he had a significant-other and multiple-children in their household.

As we had started to talk and be amiable, his story started to be revealed. This Marine had been through a version of hell, and it was apparent early on after hearing about some of his challenges there was a reason we had connected, and that Impact Montana was going to have a role in his eventual pursuit to thrive. I say eventual because thriving was the last thing on his mind at many points early on in our connection.

A significant part of this Marine's journey is that he had been in an explosion that resulted in his best friend being killed and him enduring brain and physical injuries from the blast. This was a situation not only with a result of post-traumatic stress, but it was likely a case of moral injury as well.

As we started the process of walking through his challenges, it was apparent that God needed to be an integral part of his recovery and was undoubtedly a part of our connection. No matter how hard he tried, he continued to tread water. Between the prescription medications and other personal choices, the challenges continued, eventually being involuntarily dismissed from his home for conduct detrimental to his family. In addition to the separation, this Marine had experienced homelessness, addiction, unemployment, significant depression, and suicidal thoughts.

All along, even in the darkest of days for this Marine, God was there to promote spiritual growth and healing. This was not only in his life but in his significant other's life as well. Despite their relationship challenges, I trust his significant other and family stayed true to their faith by praying for their relationship and him. Almost two years later, it is evident that this is the case.

My role as a mentor was to be a strong voice for Jesus and to promote spiritual healing, health and wellness, and recovery. Along with connecting him to therapeutic modalities that would be beneficial for the injuries and Mighty Oaks, a Christian peer-to-peer resilience and recovery program, it was my obligation to simply be there to offer guidance and pray for his ability to thrive.

When I had returned from my recent deployment, his family had no longer lived across the street from my family. And his family was still without him. But over a few months, reconciliation had begun between the Marine and his significant other and their children. The prescriptions had been minimized. Counseling with the local vet center continued, and interaction with God became more than just a Sunday event.

Since the reconciliation, this Marine is not only back with his family, but his family has also purchased a home together. And he is engaged to be married to this woman, a woman who has emulated God by offering tremendous grace and unconditional love.

This story is how I came to realize Impact Montana's wellness pillars were more than just placeholders for programming. In our relationship prompted by his need for a strong mentor, it became evident that by focusing on all of these facets, or thrive factors, an individual would increase their ability to grow and ultimately thrive. No matter where the Marine was, God was there, and so was I as an unconditional friend and mentor.

God-ordained relationships like the one just shared have been arranged in accordance with God's will. They are not set in conditions, and when a need arises, the other person's obligation is to recognize their role as a servant and ambassador for Jesus. The stronger our faith grows, the easier it is to see which relationships are intended to be more than for just our benefit. And at the end of the day, the benefit is not only for the individual being mentored, but most certainly the mentor as well.

It is important to note that not all friendships are of this magnitude, and it is important to honor the importance of boundaries and be well-rounded socially in order to thrive socially.

RECREATION WITH PEERS

When I personally think of thriving socially, I think pointedly of what I would have considered it to look like many years ago: playing golf with three of my best friends, driving hundreds of miles to watch a college basketball tournament, spending the day on a boat on a Montana lake, or perhaps vacationing with friends in a land far, far away. While these are viable means to help one thrive socially, thriving socially is more about the relationships than it is about the activities.

I know several groups of guys who float a specific river in Montana on an annual basis, and I will heed to the notion that their experiences carry more value relative to the group of guys that they are floating and sharing the experience with and less on the activity itself. The river just happens to be the bonus.

Thriving socially through recreation is not necessarily a conditioner for impact, meaning recreational activities are not a contributing factor to the capacity of impact. In fact, it can offer negative value if it interferes with being able to create margin for no-compromise factors.

What it does contribute to when given its due, is stress relief or decompression from what tends to be busy lifestyles. And when we don't prioritize extracurricular activities, we end up decreasing our capacity for thriving and impact because of the increased and unrelieved pressure.

One of the most often used excuses that is heard when discussing potential recreational or extracurricular activities is that "I am too busy." Busy is an excuse that allows us to justify being disconnected from our peer group and ultimately thriving socially.

The problem is that busy has become an idol in our culture and we glorify being busy.

> *Gold Nugget: Busy is this new sexy symbol that says we are important or that there are different priorities than the given opportunity, but in reality, the gauge for what indicates our importance should correlate with our capacity for impact. And if we are not creating margin and prioritizing decompression and stress relief by doing the things we love to do with those who we enjoy being around, we decrease our capacity for thriving and impact.*

So while I will discuss later functional capacity and how capacity for impact is drastically reduced by margin lost through excessive extracurricular activities, it is important to note now that finding an appropriate work/life balance will contribute to the energy necessary to thrive.

THRIVE FACTOR 6: FINANCIAL HEALTH

"One pretends to be rich, yet has nothing; another pretends to be poor, yet has great wealth" (Proverbs 13:7).

I am not ashamed to admit that I have been at rock bottom in each of the thrive factors, but especially in financial wellness. Part of my motivation for writing this book is to share my journey and trust that someone will benefit from learning from my brokenness. And through my journey, one thing I have learned is that being at rock bottom financially for me was more significantly related to being spiritually broken than it is relative to being financially broke.

Gold Nugget: One can have very little in terms of wealth yet be incredibly rich spiritually, just like one can have incredible wealth and be spiritually bankrupt with no hope for eternity.

As I have shown in all of the other previously mentioned thrive factors, the point again here is that in order to thrive financially and live in impact, there is a direct correlation to spiritual health.

Possession being 90 percent of the law is a popular mantra in our society, with the idea that someone who owns something and has it in their possession is the rightful responsible party for that something; however, scripturally speaking, the notion is that Christians are instead bound by God's law and that everything we have is not actually ours. But if we treat it as ours, we miss the opportunity to bless others and more importantly be a blessing to God.

It is easier said than done, but money, home, and kids need to be released from the clenched grip, and when that happens, there is tremendous spiritual freedom. All of our resources and wealth (family included) are to be treated as a blessing to God, not a means for personal possession.

While I only offer biblically based mentorship when I am working with someone who is struggling in various facets of their lives, there is genuinely only one tenet I offer that can assist with financial management. And because I am not a certified personal financial counselor, it is my personal recommendation for anyone struggling financially to connect with a faith-based financial management program if this is an area in your life needing to get a grip on.

The tenet I share is centered on managing the financial resources one is responsible for, a plan for the income one makes, and living within the means of that income with margin. From my perspective, thriving financially is really that simple.

Impact is thwarted with heavy debt, vehicles, homes, and other toys that not only drain our financial resources but other resources as well. Neither impact nor thriving comes from living frivolously and without intention. Impact and thriving instead come from aligning our investing in opportunities and engaging in generosity adjacent to our financial plan and values.

The spiritual wellness component of this is being protected from impulsivity, resource mismanagement, and getting-rich-quick schemes, all of which I have fallen victim to. Just like when there is a significant spiritual transformation in one's life, the lessons learned through the journey make the mistakes invaluable. The hard lessons make the victories glorious.

VALUES-BASED INVESTING

When I hear the word "investing" or "investment," I don't think of the typical opportunity to put money into a mutual fund or get into the stock market, hoping for a big return on a new and upcoming company. Instead I think specifically of aligning my financial resources with business opportunities that coincide with my values, and I also think of supporting nonprofit organizations and faith-based ministries that do the same. In fact, this is a no-compromise proposition.

I have as a Christian committed to only placing my money into opportunities and businesses that are first and foremost values-centric. The residual effect of this is that typically an organization with strong values will treat their employees, customers, and additional stakeholders well, thus offering a modest return. I am always willing to support this type of business.

The no-compromise proposition means that I will refrain from investing our family's resources, that we manage for God, into a business strictly to potentially receive a high financial return. It is always a matter of values over financial reward. This is an area that I strongly recommend all Christians prayerfully consider, and frankly it takes some digging into to identify who and what is tied to potential investments.

Having been involved in helping facilitate Dave Ramsey's *Financial Peace University* for several years, I would consider Mr. Ramsey a pseudo-mentor, just by listening to his podcasts and utilizing most of his financial management principles. One thing that has resonated with me the most through this experience is that with pursuing financial wellness comes the choice of seeking financial prosperity, or we have the alternative option of managing our God-given resources according to our values and building impact that is bigger than us, a contributing factor for creating our legacy.

Thriving holistically does not allow us to pursue optimal health, family wellness, a purposeful career, and dynamic social connections and then compromise on our faith in order to return a high profit to increase our personal wealth. Being influential and leaving a mark for Jesus means thriving spiritually and that all other facets of thriving will coincide with godly pursuit.

GENEROSITY AND GIVING

This is the perfect culmination point for the thrive factors discussion. When it comes to financially thriving, it is the financial plan, or how the money is proactively managed, that I have indicated is the key to success. The integral component to having a plan that has a direct correlation to thriving spiritually and living influentially is how generosity and giving are prioritized in the plan. Biblically speaking, we are to give our first fruits to the church, not as a result of the margin available after all other obligations have been met.

If you go back to the definition of what impact is in the first chapter, you will see that the definition fits into our responsibility to be generous and give. The quickest way to live in impact is to be generous and give to the point that others see the light of Jesus through your actions. Spiritually speaking, there is no greater opportunity to be a blessing to God than to be generous and a giver relative to Christian values, as generosity is a strong indicator of love.

Generosity and giving are not limited to financially contributing to the church or a particular cause; generosity and giving can and should also emulate volunteering, as was seen in the career thrive factor section.

If there is any part of the thrive factors and my experience specifically that I pray resonates with you, it is the notion that when we think we have life all figured out and are managing it according to our will, our capacity is limited. We might find personal success. We might be happy some of the time, but we are still missing something. There is a void in our souls because we have not reached our full potential spiritually, which we won't actually do until we are glorified in heaven. The desires of our heart while we are here on earth, our soul purpose, cannot be filled without the hope and reliance that is only found through a relationship with Jesus Christ.

Now that we have wrapped up the thrive factors, we can continue moving forward and look at the principles that will help generate the impact that one may be chasing.

CHAPTER 5

OPERATING AT FUNCTIONAL CAPACITY

"NOT THAT I AM SPEAKING of being in need, for I have learned in whatever situation I am to be content. I know how to be brought low, and I know how to abound. In any and every circumstance I have learned the secret of facing plenty and hunger, abundance and need. I can do all things through him who strengthens me" (Philippians 4:11–13 ESV).

The last part of the verse above from Philippians 4 is a powerful representation of maximizing functional capacity. Notice it does not say, "I can do all things with my own strength." Paul is articulating the vastness of the capacity of strength that is increased when we leverage what has been given to us. It is not about us in so many ways. It is about what Jesus has done for us, which supernaturally and spiritually propels us to new heights.

Part of my motivation to write this book has come from my interest in personal and professional growth, and naturally wanting to share how faith contributes to both. In the dichotomy that is the world and living for Jesus, we are oftentimes inundated with internal conflict when it comes to personal development. But heeding to faith instead of the world when it comes to our growth is vital for our journey.

The idea of functional capacity is relatively simple. It is the idea that we all have a maximum output in which we can perform, but many don't meet our functional capacity because we limit our capabilities by not leveraging God. If Jesus can turn water into wine, raise Lazarus from the dead, and feed five thousand people with a loaf of bread, he certainly can influence our output, or functional capacity.

Functional capacity comes from a combination of our skills, intellectual capabilities, physical prowess, and/or, most importantly, source and connection to soul purpose. You can likely sense a strong theme at this point (Galatians 2:20).

Our spiritual health has the ability to decrease the wasted margin between our actual level of performance from skills, intellect, or physical abilities and increase our level of performance with an injection of strength gained from Christ to reach our functional capacity. You and I have limits, but Jesus died for us on the cross to shatter our own personal limits (in more ways than one) and to help us outperform our limits so others can see God's glory.

Without faith and the perspective it offers, we are bound to our own limitations, whereas faith and the desire to be better than our limitations with spiritual connectivity assist in reaching our functional capacity. Contextually speaking, the only way to increase our functional capacity and impact is to be strengthened in our relationship with Jesus and live in a new identity, which comes through daily spiritual disciplines.

In my professional work, I have found that not leveraging God causes people to think smaller than they would if God was actually in the picture. The problem with this is significant in that thinking small produces small results.

Believe it or not, we have individuals in the US military that dread doing a physical fitness test, which exponentially limits their functional capacity. Instead of thinking about just passing the test, they could increase their capacity simply by considering their soul purpose behind having a physically fit body that is ready and able to do well on the test under any condition, giving them the conditioning to perform at increased levels in times of incredible stress, like war. Dreading the test limits the value that can come out of its benefits. The inability to recognize the value of being physically fit for a purpose is an indication of less-than-optimal spiritual health.

Consider the notion that our soul purpose is simply influencing how God can receive the glory through whatever we are doing. So physical training is honoring God by being in the best physical conditioning we can be for a purpose, which in the military example means being physically fit, resilient, and always being ready for battle. The reasons are going to be relative, but as long as they are for God's benefit and not our own personal pleasure or gain, we are supernaturally able to increase our functional capacity.

I think one of the best and little known examples of leveraging God to increase personal functional capacity in the Bible (that is not of Jesus) is found in 2 Samuel 23:20, where Benaiah's heroic feats are recorded.

If you are not familiar with Benaiah, I strongly encourage you to study this man as he is a wonderful example of a spiritual warrior who maxed out his functional capacity by killing lions and men who posed lionlike threats. This is a great account of God doing with his kingdom what he wants and a human's functional capacity increasing because of God.

Had Benaiah not been obedient to his call, he would have never been able to survive long enough to witness God's plan for King David's son Solomon to become his predecessor as king; because he was obedient though, he was able to contribute mightily to God's work.

I will not be the first in line to go toe to toe against a lion like Benaiah did; however, more often than not, it is realized that if I am in a precarious place (as I do my best to limit my time with lions one on one), it is because I trust that God has brought me to the situation for his purpose, so the only way through it is with him. It is our spiritual health and faith in Jesus that will always increase our functional capacity. But what about limiting it?

As we saw with the thrive factors, there may be toxic behaviors or relationships that will limit our capacity, not to mention that we carry our own limitations.

Gold Nugget: We can have a limited and maxed-out functional capacity because we have too many toxins in our lives. When this is the case, it is essential that we identify and remove the toxins and create margin to support our ability to thrive. Creating margins will never come without a cost. It may be at someone else's cost, it may be at a personal cost of pleasure or comfort, or it may even be a financial cost. Nonetheless, functional capacity will always be limited without constant assessment of margin relative to our prescription to thrive.

CREATING WHITE SPACE

The white space I speak of here is what is also referred to as margin throughout the book. I like the term "white space" because it indicates that there is nothing there, or theoretically it is room to breathe. In the fast-paced world we live in, it is vital we create space that we do not have obligations, responsibilities, mandates, and so forth and allow ourselves the ability to slow down and count our blessings.

For much of my professional career and life as a dad, my time traveling or driving across Montana has served as my white space, or margin. Even though driving by myself for work purposes long distances still requires the need to be fully aware of the situation and things going on around me, it still affords opportunity to reduce chaos and appreciate all of the good that God has blessed me and my family with. There is a purpose associated with maximizing available white space.

Being busy, as I have already mentioned, is to a fault a significant contributing factor that limits our ability to thrive. Idolizing busy instead of placing significant value on margin will negatively influence the most important relationships in our lives. When we have margin, we have the ability to allow opportunity for the most important things to be a part of our lives. This is not only the case for relationships, but it also is the case for all of the other thrive factors as well; therefore, creating margin and focusing on the most important conditions in our thrive factors assessment helps us with the process of developing our thrive action plan, or prescription to thrive.

THRIVE ACTION PLAN

Barriers that prevent or limit an individual's ability to thrive or live in impact are directly related to identifying and effectively managing what areas limit and produce energy relative to the identified thrive factors. Based on the results of the thrive factors assessment, an effort can then take place to create a plan that will help an individual thrive. And just like a fingerprint, the thrive action plan will be unique to each individual yet can only be developed by asking two important questions: What am I not willing to give up (no-compromise) because it is a part of my soul purpose? What am I willing to give up (compensation factors) that will allow me (and potentially others with me) to create a margin for alternative factors that assist in promoting the ability to thrive?

1. No-compromise: As you have seen throughout this book, I have identified several areas in my personal ability to thrive as no-compromise factors, all predicated on seeing life through that faith-based lens. The intention with this is to identify the things in life that are most important and

contribute to the ability to promote thriving. The idea is not to create a complete thrive action plan based on no-compromise factors, but instead to recognize and prioritize the most valuable components in the thrive action plan. The no-compromise factors will essentially be the part of the plan that helps the individual or family heed to their values, mission statement, and soul purpose.

For example, a family with three kids with different extracurricular activities such as sports, dance, music lessons, and 4-H on a limited income is going to have to make some hard decisions in order to accommodate the interests of the children and family. It may be necessary to find an additional source of income to support these interests or to cut back and put energy toward activities and interests that are more purposeful than others and with less cost. In the situation where a family wants each of their kids involved in the activities, there is no-compromise or willingness to give up the activities, so the family simply determines how they are going to support all of the extracurricular activities.

Because the context of this book and the theories in it are built on living in soul purpose and its connection to impact, the no-compromise factors being encouraged are biblically based and afford no alteration. We simply cannot compromise on anything that contributes to our soul purpose.

Compromising faith will lead to changing the way other factors are pursued, like justifying actions for pleasure instead of purpose. Compromising other factors without compromising faith keeps us in the purview of soul purpose and on track for impact.

Jesus called his disciples to leave what they were doing to follow him, which at the surface may seem extreme, but in reality, when we turn our lives over to Jesus Christ and confess that we are full of sin and that he as our Savior is the only way to be forgiven of sin, this is the exact same pursuit we are committing to. We are committing to pursuing and following Jesus and his destiny for our lives and walking away from our own personal pleasures and desires.

2. Compensation factor: Just like we have to identify and prioritize factors that align us with our soul purpose, in the thrive action plan it is also necessary to identify factors taking up margin and hold less value than other factors that are positively contributing factors to energy production. This can be a spiritual assessment of whether something is being pursued for pleasure or if there is purposeful value attributed to it.

    Every choice made affords compromise from an alternate option. Think about the significance of habitually poor decision-making and how easy it is to have your brain be stuck in that mode. Typically this occurs because there is a subconsciously perceived value of immediate pleasure associated with the choice made, but in reality, this pleasure is temporary, and a compromise is made against doing something good, or purposeful.

    Now consider your options to get out of your negative actions and bad choice pattern. In order to make good decisions, you must know good, which will eventually allow one to be good. Knowing God's Word and his goodness affords physical change in the brain, resulting in being able to conform to the goodness of God. Mitigating circumstances can certainly affect this ability for our brains to comprehend, but because God is good, we have access to his goodness. Conforming to God's goodness and our soul purpose allows us to determine where there is opportunity to increase margin. Aligning with pleasure over purpose will always limit our impact when we are not able or willing to align the pleasure with purpose.

    For example, if my love for golf keeps me on the golf course eight hours a week and costs several thousands of dollars a year, I have to weigh the costs relative to what it is taking away from my family. Essentially, unless I am getting paid to golf, which is certainly not my case, I am compromising family values, both relationally and financially, for my personal pleasure.

Needless to say, I gave up golf for the most part several years ago because I recognized the negative value at the rate I was playing and what it would produce over the long term. In reality, despite the perceived loss I incurred from golf due to the love I have for the game, it was actually a gain because it had contributed zero value to my soul purpose once I had a family. This is not to say that golf will not serve a purpose in my life someday, but as it goes right now, there are higher priorities that I have chosen over golf.

A great example of this is choosing to give up or limit a passion that contributes negative value, both financial and spiritual (like golf for me), personally and replace it with doing something with the family that will create value like memories that will last a lifetime.

Unfortunately families get torn apart at the seams because one or both of the adults in the family are not willing to give up something that gives them personal pleasure over something that is purposeful for their family. When there is an unwillingness to give up something with negative value to the rest of the family, it will more often than not lead to a break-up of the family.

Before my journey of faith started, there was only one thing that was being chased, pleasure. Then at the point when faith in God became a part of my journey, functional capacity increased, and the pursuit became about others and glorifying God instead of personal desires and pleasure. Naturally there was a shift in margin being filled more with purpose and less with pleasure.

Part of the intent of the thrive factors assessment is to create margin by determining no-compromise factors and negotiating factors that contribute little to no value with factors of higher value that contribute to thriving and align with purposeful pursuit. So where do we begin to fill in the margin when we have identified the margin to manage?

The first step is knowing that we have responsibilities, desires, and things that are no-compromise or that we are not willing to give up despite not being a responsibility or desire. Determining priorities starts with identifying purposeful action versus doing something for pleasure, or personal gain. When there is a conflict, the choice is simple: no-compromise factors and responsibilities always come before desires, and desires are suitable only when there is value to them.

Giving further credence to margin, we see a prime example and the value of it with Jesus "often" (Luke 5:16) escaping to the wilderness in order to pray, which indicates the priority that we need to place on creating margin for this reason. We don't necessarily need to escape to the wilderness; however, many, including me, find solitude in being close to the wilderness for accomplishing this exact purpose. Margin, or white space, in and of itself was a contributing factor for Jesus's ability to thrive, and it can also support our ability to thrive.

Before we move on, it is necessary to mention the fact that when I speak of the delineation between pleasure and purpose, pleasure is not always negative. The value associated with pleasure will be directly measured relative to its purpose. There can be value in pleasure if the factor is a contribution toward purpose. For example, someone who gets pleasure out of their career can certainly be contributing to their soul purpose. In fact, it should be this way; however, when it takes away from one's ability to contribute to their soul purpose, there is negative value, and the need then exists to determine where changes should be made.

CHAPTER 6

GENERATIONALLY EXCLUSIVE

> Knowing that you were ransomed from the futile ways
> inherited from your forefathers, not with perishable things
> such as silver or gold, but with the precious blood of Christ,
> like that of a lamb without blemish or spot.
> —1 Peter 1:18-19

IF THE THRIVE ACTION PLAN is the prescription that can help someone thrive, I will also suggest that the definition of "impact" I shared previously is a prescription for creating a legacy. And just like impact, legacy is not about us or how we personally will benefit. Legacy is about contributing to something bigger than self; it is evidence of a life lived in soul purpose and deflecting personal glory for what has been or will be accomplished and giving God the glory for it. If you want to establish your legacy, how you live first and foremost has to be spiritual or God-centric, purposeful, and change the trajectory, or course, for your family, community, nation, or generation (Deuteronomy 6:1–8).

In my experience working professionally, I have found that the two biggest obstacles for any person to influence their legacy is their generational bondage and bondage to sin that exists.

As we see in Deuteronomy 6, the commands that are given are all centered on God; thus if the genetic line before us were not faithful following Jesus, there is a disconnect from the knowledge of God and a deeper connection to genetic predisposition and personal experiences. Oftentimes we aren't even aware of these spiritual barriers that impede our ability to influence our legacy.

The world says legacy is a gift or something of value that is handed down or transferred to a subsequent generation; however, Christian legacy is determined by the value of the passing down to others the relationship between the subject and Jesus reflective in testimony and discipleship. Legacy is in direct relationship to adherence to soul purpose and impact.

As Christians, we are not bound to our genes or generations who have come before us or our past failures or transgressions, but instead bound to the grace, love, and hope found through Jesus Christ. This can be a hard concept to grasp for nonbelievers and even sometimes believers depending on the denomination of Christian faith. It is not until someone understands grace and the atonement of sin that will allow them to comprehend fully the significance of being able to break this bondage.

It is important to note that despite getting caught up in a desire to leave a financial legacy, the priority for legacy needs to be spiritual. A financial gift without understanding how to use it for God's benefit is simply a gift without purpose. But a financial gift from a Christian who has left their mark by loving others through their words and deeds offers more eternal value through their faith than through a financial gift. Biblical principles like work ethic, financial management, family support, gaining wisdom, and so forth hold eternal value and more worth than temporal gain.

When I think of legacy, I think of my wife's grandfather. I did not have the opportunity to spend much time getting to know him as he was in his late seventies when I met him. But the time I did have with him left an impression on me like no other man I have ever known personally. I could sit and listen to him tell stories for hours if given the opportunity because his character shined bright through his storytelling.

He was a sailor who served in World War II, so we shared

that service connection, but it was so much more than that. Everything he had come to know in life was developed relative to his soul purpose. There was eternal value in every aspect of his life. The hardships were purposeful, the relationships were fruitful, his love for hunting and fishing was unmatched, work experiences were rewarding, and certainly his faith all held incredible spiritual value.

Even with all of this, nothing mattered more to him than his relationship with Jesus, and everything else rested on that. If there were no connection to soul purpose and being able to have Jesus revealed in what he was doing, it was not going to be a part of his life. In essence, his functional capacity was maximized because he did not compromise on things of eternal value. The greatest mark he left on the world is the love he had for Jesus and the influence generationally he had on those who follow him.

GENERATIONAL BONDAGE

My dad, by worldly definition, is sort of your all-American male figure. Growing up, I had what many would consider a hero as a father. He played and excelled at college football, and then by the time I was old enough to understand anything about my parents, I understood that he was the part-owner of one of two health clubs in our hometown. These were certainly two things I was proud of my dad the most.

What I did not understand was that there was a void in his heart that caused him to chase pleasure more than impact. Unfortunately the kind of impact I have been attempting to articulate was at his full disposal. He had tremendous opportunity to influence many lives in this context, but the opportunity fell short primarily because pleasure was prioritized over impact.

I hold no personal grudges against my dad and while he was still alive walked alongside him as much as I could as he navigated through the end of life with dementia and loneliness. The reality of the situation is that up until I had a relationship with Jesus I was not far behind him in my pursuit of pleasure.

This pursuit of pleasure for me resulted in hurt relationships, financial despair, addiction, and an intense loneliness that also left a void in my heart. For a long time, I had bondage to my dad and an anger that was a result of thinking I was destined to be him for the rest of my life.

I wanted to emulate my dad so much growing up that I worked at the health club he was part owner of, sometimes thinking and acting like I already owned the place, and also at one of the local beverage distributorships where he was a salesman.

It wasn't until during my first deployment that I got away from Montana, away from chasing pleasure and in a warzone, where the meaning of life is assessed daily, that I came to grips with the fact that I needed to make some significant life changes when I returned to the United States. For the first time in my life, I was doing something that my dad had not done, something of perceived value, serving my country in war.

In 2006, I wrote a letter to my dad while I was in Little Rock, Arkansas, for a military school. I wrote to him about these grudges I had against him and how it spoiled our relationship and the ill feelings I had for him in my heart. In that letter, I also forgave him and told him it was only possible because I now had an understanding of where perfect love came from and what it meant to me to be loved by God with this perfect love (Romans 8:28–30).

My expectations of my dad had shifted because I realized he was who he was, which was not someone who would be able to give me the kind of love each one of us deserves. I could only receive that kind of love from my heavenly Father and his Son Jesus Christ who laid down his life for us (John 15:13). For the first time in my life, I was separated from the generational chain and living in the sins of my biological father; instead I found peace and security living in the grace of our heavenly Father.

Not only do we want to be aware of how our generational

chains from our parents are influential in our lives, but we also want to be careful not to be bound to our children's successes or failures. Yes, we want to see them be active, intelligent, and successful in their pursuits, but we don't want to be bound to these things that can be detrimental to our ability to give God the glory he deserves.

Many people regardless of faith find themselves in similar situations. We get caught up in the successes or failures, the wealth or notoriety, or the social influence of our parents, which biblically speaking are generational sin, as the idolatry in things other than God prevents us from having the relationship with him that he desires.

If your question is how we start releasing the generational bondage, we should start first with prayerfully reflecting on the grip we feel our parents or family members have on our destiny and go to scripture and seek guidance on what God wants from us.

Being bound to our parents or children is an unintentional gifting of glory to them, which naturally robs God of the glory he is seeking from us. And because God is a jealous God, we don't want to take away what is rightfully his.

This bondage that can be created generationally has power over our ability to follow Jesus as he commanded. Jesus was very strict in his orders to follow him, and the applicability remains the same today (Matthew 8:18–22). When Jesus denied one of the disciples in his desire to bury his father, the denial was a point being made that living for him actually meant that the priority was now him, and he had broken away from the generational bondage but was bound to his responsibility in following Jesus.

While there is a bondage that can be found through generational sin, we may also be bound to personal sin. They are not mutually exclusive in that if we break generational bondage, we can still be bound by personal sin.

BONDAGE OF SIN

Gold Nugget: We cannot change our current situation, but we can change our perception and ability to respond in our situation. We cannot change the past, but we can change us to be better in the future.

When we are unable to separate from our past, whether it is good or bad, we are held in bondage, which jeopardizes our future. This sin I speak of from the past could be through self-glorification (stuck in our glory years), or it could be a result of the acts of sin of the flesh, such as what the apostle Paul speaks of in Galatians 5. Paul's warning to avoid giving in to the desires of the flesh (sin) are protected by the Holy Spirit. Earlier in this passage, Paul is praising the freedom that comes from Jesus; yet this freedom he speaks of is not the freedom that one may think it is, as the freedom to do whatever we want to do would be counterintuitive to living a life in Christ. Instead Paul is encouraging freedom by being delivered through the love of Jesus.

What happens when the sin includes taking away God's glory for the sake of owning it ourselves? Perhaps better stated, minimizing our own sin in order to maximize our own glory? If our primary obligation, our soul purpose, as Christians is to praise and honor God, which is an activator for impact, we are compromising living in impact for our own glory. We can't be living in our own glory and chasing impact at the same time. Even as Christians, if Christ is not our focal point for impact, we have failed in our utmost responsibility of giving God glory.

For believers and nonbelievers alike, not many like to indulge in conversations about sin. But for Christians, the reality is that we recognize that we are sinners, yet only because of Christ's grace and love for us, we are saved from our sin and have access to God the Father in heaven. So sin does not have the same weight for us as it does for nonbelievers.

For one that is bound to sin because Christ and his free gift of grace have not been received, the consequences are severe. In Christ, there is no bondage, but outside of Christ, death will be forevermore. The freedom found in Christ is the freedom that separates us from all bondage and all sin. We cannot be bound to sin when we have embraced the freedom gained from the cross.

For further understanding of the significance of sin and freedom found in Christ, I encourage you to take a journey down the Romans road to salvation by studying the apostolic work of Paul in the book of Romans.

In summary, glory is either going to be given to our parents or children (unrightfully), ourselves (unrightfully), or God, and if we can't give credit where it is due, we are simply falling short of our responsibility of living out our faith (James 2:14–26).

CHAPTER 7

ENHANCED THROUGH EXPERIENCE

> It is not the critic who counts; not the man who points out
> how the strong man stumbles, or where the doer of deeds
> could have done them better. The credit belongs to the man
> who is actually in the arena, whose face is marred by dust and
> sweat and blood; who strives valiantly; who errs, who comes
> short again and again, because there is no effort without
> error and shortcoming; but who does actually strive to do
> the deeds; who knows great enthusiasms, the great devotions;
> who spends himself in a worthy cause; who at the best knows
> in the end the triumph of high achievement, and who at the
> worst, if he fails, at least fails while daring greatly, so that
> his place shall never be with those cold and timid souls who
> neither know victory nor defeat.
> —Teddy Roosevelt, "Man in the Arena"

WHAT WOULD HAPPEN IF WE as parents took a trip with
our kids to a country that is unlike what we are used to here in
America? Granted, many of the developed countries across the
world have been Westernized and look similar to our culture;
however, even being introduced to a new culture at ten years old
when I traveled to Europe with a boys' choir and then again in 2002
and 2003 for our National Guard annual training, I was introduced

to a whole new culture, certainly different than what I was used to with life here in the United States.

I think further about the fact that if we as parents took our kids to Third World countries to support missions, how life-changing that would be for not only our kids but us as adults as well. Or it may even be as simple as coordinating work on an Indian reservation in our home state or working with inner-city youth to help gain an understanding of how others unlike us live.

This is probably a topic to be reserved for another day, but some of the most oppressed people we have the closest proximity to share the gospel with are shortsighted opportunities because we fail in living out Jesus's command to go out into the world, discipling and baptizing others in the name of Jesus Christ.

I contend that we do a poor job of expanding our scope, or perspective, by limiting our perspectives to our own experiences and education, driving our emotional responses to societal challenges and levels that drive division from those who do not share the same perspective as us.

Living amongst and serving the most vulnerable and sharing the love of Christ is one of the most powerful means to enhance perspective and genuinely build the understanding of how people unlike us live. We are not called to only serve those who are with privilege, but instead to serve the less fortunate, including orphans, widows, or brothers and sisters without basic necessities (James 1:27).

Many in the church are bound to limited perspectives because we have not ventured outside our comfort zone to see where ministry is needed. Unfortunately this is a validation of one's faith as we are to be mindful of and live out the gospel where our brothers and sisters need compassion the most.

People in general are more invested in the easy instead of getting dirty, which includes those professing to be Christians. This I don't believe to be a fault of anyone specifically, but instead bred by our very own society.

> *Gold Nugget: Living in the easy separates us from impact, keeps us living in pleasure instead of purpose, and minimizes value through experience.*

Looking back on the eighteen-year-old me and derived from my childhood upbringing, I had skewed expectations. As mentioned earlier, my expectations consisted of going to college, getting a degree, finding the woman of my dreams, getting my dream job, having kids, and living happily ever after. The expectations were horribly interrupted after my first semester of college and facing the reality that the things I wanted in life were going to have to be worked hard for. Imagine that.

The reality of my situation was that because I had never faced difficult circumstances, had most of what I wanted in life given to me, and did not know the value of hard work, life was going to be more difficult than I was prepared to contribute to. Because I was not allowed to experience failure, I was not able to manage failure down the road. This is why experiencing failure along with successes is so important. Now many years later, I embrace failure and more specifically the opportunities learned from it because I know there is purpose in it.

At the time, failure can be painful, especially when we think what we were pursuing aligns with our impact, or purpose. But when this occurs, there is a spiritual awakening in that we recognize that it was not in fact a part of our purpose, or if it is, we will see it come to fruition outside of the time we anticipated it occurring. Regardless of the source, pain can serve significant value when it is renamed and given meaning and purpose.

I already shared previously about my experience going through the chaplain candidate process and being denied the opportunity to serve as a chaplain after the first accessioning board. Rather than trust the process and know that God had full authority over my ability to serve as a chaplain, I was still caught up in the failure of the experience thinking that I had more control than I actually had.

Another significant life experience that has played an instrumental role in my life was an adoption that did not take place as we thought it was supposed to be our responsibility and purpose. After a few years of attempting to have children, my wife and I were asked if we would adopt a family friend's baby that was to be born. With prayer, despite my initial personal hesitation, we accepted the call and started the process of intrastate adoption. And much to our dismay, the mother retreated on her intention and decided she was going to challenge the state of Washington in order to keep her baby.

At the time, we had a hard time figuring out why this adoption failed, but in reality, it was not failure. It was a disillusion and ultimately a blessing as later that year we found out that my wife was pregnant.

If this is not an indication of our need to trust God's plan, I am not sure what is. And if we were not faithful followers of Jesus, we may not recognize this as part of his story and just chalk it up to chance or not make anything out of it at all.

EMBRACING FAILURE

Some of my most influential moments in my life have come from failure. I know not many would admit that, and even for me, it is humbling to say, but the most valuable learning experiences of my adult life have all been derived from failure, but they have been nothing short of influential, largely from their ability to be constructive and not destructive.

These learning experiences all have something in common. That common thread is that instead of giving in to the failure, the failure was used to motivate or to propel forward, leveraging the experience to make the degree of impact greater.

We have the choice and ability to limit the effect that failure has on our lives by considering the role that the failure had; and just like the resources we manage for God, it is our ability to manage failure for God that will make it purposeful. These failures could have very easily stopped me in my path, but that would be completely neglecting the role that God plays in my life. Unfortunately many of the individuals I have worked with have let failure be very destructive, ultimately defeating them, oftentimes minimizing the ability to move past the failure.

Challenges that come about through failed experiences keeping someone from moving forward are similar to the bondage we discussed previously resulting in destruction instead of growth and is evidence that an individual places too much value on self and not enough value on God. The inability to learn from the past means that one cannot separate themselves from the past and find opportunity in it, regardless of its success or failure.

There is a strong faith component to this, which means that the value received from the experience is in direct correlation to the spiritual health of the individual going through the experience or who has lived in the experience. And the stumbling blocks or obstacles to impact can be deemed unresolved conflicts of the heart or mismanaged emotions and response from the experience. The inability to manage emotions, allowing the failure to be destructive, will prevent someone from thriving and living in impact.

If faith is a tie that binds one's ability to thrive, as was determined previously, then I would agree with Special Forces Officer, Lieutenant Colonel Scott Mann, and the notion that struggle is "a universal singular that binds us" and that "scars are a mark on the soul" (*Generosity of Scars*). Let's face it. Life is hard, and we all face hardships, but those hardships don't have to be what defines us. Suffering is universal, yes, but the path that each of us takes to journey through suffering is unique to the person's capacity to live in the value of suffering.

PTSD VERSUS PTSG

We are going to take a little bit of a detour in our conversation and talk about trauma. Clearly put, failure can certainly be traumatic, but trauma is not always a result of failure. And because there is much that is written on trauma that will not be addressed in this book, we will limit our focus to the effects on the spiritual health side of trauma, which can also be deemed moral injury. Spiritual health will either contribute to stress from trauma leading to disorder, also known as PTSd, or post-traumatic stress disorder, or it can cause the trauma to lead to growth, or PTSG.

Just like the relationship between trauma and failure identified previously, trauma has a unique relationship with moral injury, whereas there can be moral injury as a result of trauma; however, moral injury does not always occur when there is a traumatic event. Moral injury is more related to the individual's disconnect from a moral construct than the severity of the trauma.

If an individual who grew up in the church understanding a loving, yet punishing, God goes into military service and is victim to military sexual trauma, while having the perpetrator walk away without punishment from military justice channels, then rightfully so that individual may have a crisis of faith.

Not only did the punitive system fail this individual, but the perception may be that this loving God failed them as well by allowing this to happen, all the while not taking into consideration the universe that God rules over.

When a Christian overcomes and experiences personal growth through trauma, the reason would be because the focus was never taken off God and the traumatic event never got bigger than the trust one has in God, resulting in PTSG, or post-traumatic stress growth. But when the trauma becomes PTSd and often moral injury, it is because the traumatic event became stronger than the perceived value of an incongruent God.

I am going to be blunt in saying that the church overall has failed in its ability to address moral injury, which in fact can be reasonably assumed is a reason that many once-professing Christians have walked away from the church. If we cannot have a conversation about trauma and help someone reconcile it biblically, then how can we expect anyone who is not able to reconcile their trauma to stay strong in their faith? This is where the church should be drawing people to and transforming people in Christ as the only construct in which to stake claim to morality in is the Bible. And if the Bible is not in the midst of attempting to help someone reconcile their trauma, there can be no moral reconciliation.

For a biblical representation of what this looks like, we have the book of Job, a testament to the complexity of suffering and how much we tend to put the ability to survive through it on our own shoulders. The dialogue between Job and God was not satisfying to Job as he was not receiving the response he wanted from God regarding his suffering from incredible loss. In turn, Job's trust waned.

Moral injury is debilitating in that it disconnects someone from their moral construct, the moral construct that is the source for all things spiritual health. And without hope, love, identity, purpose, and faith (not all-inclusive), there is the potential for someone to lose their will to fight and, God forbid, ultimately live.

We have a role to play in our capacity to survive trauma, yet because our spiritual perspective is limited and we don't have the capacity to understand the spiritual battle taking place and God's dominion over all, we as Christians get to attempt to cling to the pursuit of righteousness and submit to the almighty God in order to validate our faith, just like Job.

CHAPTER 8

SCALABLE

WE ARE ALL CHASING SOMETHING in life. The question is: what is the reality of being able to reach it? And if reached, what is the benefit for you, your family, or others? Is what you are doing today a contributing factor to reaching this objective, or is what you are doing separating you from being able to reach it? Most importantly, what is the value to God if you are able to achieve what you are pursuing?

No matter what we do or who we are, we share this commonality of pursuit. The idea that we have to have money or be of a certain status to live in impact is false. In the eyes of God, the street sweeper has as much potential for impact as does the CEO of a Fortune 500 company or the lay leader in a small community church.

The heart of *Chasing Impact* is that any person of any demographic can thrive through a prescribed set of variables, and when pursued through the lens of faith or scripture, there is in fact value to God, which at the end of the day is the most important thing we can be striving for. And out of that comes scalable impact.

> *Gold Nugget: The scalability of impact is relative to one's connection to soul purpose and their ability to use the resources that God has blessed them with in order to be a blessing to God.*

The scalability of impact is about taking what we have been blessed with, including spiritual gifts, resources, experiences, and so forth, and sharing it with others in whatever sphere of influence we have been called to be influential in. A prime example of this is seen in ministries that have been created by veterans who have been in dangerous places and done dangerous things. This can be seen simply in a local church through ministries to serve other veterans or national ministries like Mighty Oaks Warrior Programs and even global ministries like All Things Possible.

Again, this is the perfect example of God using his kingdom to minister and share the gospel on different scales. Getting to know and hear the stories of individuals like Chad Robichaux (founder of Mighty Oaks Warrior Programs), Jeremy Stalnecker (executive director of Mighty Oaks Warrior Programs), Tim Tebow (Tebow Foundation), and Victor Marx (founder of All Things Possible Ministries) has been one of the biggest blessings of my Christian life. To see the kind of impact that these men are making both nationally and globally is humbling, especially because all of their work is being done to expand the reach of the gospel, which the work they are doing is in every sense of the definition as we have been articulating, influential.

For me especially, I can fall into a comparison trap knowing that there are strong Christian ministries that are advancing the mission of the gospel. In this, my flesh falls into the desire to be like Chad, Jeremy, Tim, or Victor, but that is when I am humbled and get reconnected to the idea that we all have impact capital. We just don't all have the same scalability. Because impact is for God's benefit, it is the scalability that is up to God to determine. And measuring the scalability does not come out of the same economic system that we are used to, but instead through God's economy. Our role as Christians is to be faithful and let God place us where he needs us.

> *Gold Nugget: Despite having giant faith, sometimes it is difficult to know God doesn't need us to be the Noahs, Abrahams, Joshuas, or Pauls of the world. We just get to rest in the faith of knowing that we will be used influentially according to his needs.*

GOD'S ECONOMY

When it comes to God's economy, there is a vast difference in the management of money, time, energy, career/skills, human capital, and even relationships from a secular or societal economy. We have discussed some of this previously in the sections dedicated to the thrive factors, but it bears elaborating on as we talk about the scalability of impact.

We can do a quick comparison on how God's economy operates versus a secular economy: keeping in mind that we as Christians need to prayerfully consider the management of God's resources, which in a secular economy says that individuals are the owners of their own resources. Just like impact, as faithful followers of Jesus, none of what we possess is ours for gain, but instead it is to be managed for God's glory.

In a secular economy, the rules are fair game when personal resources like income increase, and more often than not, the gain will result in an adjustment in personal standard of living. But in God's economy, the intention for us should be to increase our standard of giving (Luke 12:34; 1 Timothy 6:17–19).

Impact, as we are discussing, at its very core, is about how well we understand what God wants from us to help him with his mission of reconciling with his people. Thus, we must seek to understand him, and the only way to connect with him for this purpose is to seek to understand by reading his Word. When we do this, we can begin to comprehend God's economy, especially concerning impact.

There is no one void of being influential in the context that we are discussing. Everyone can contribute relative to their capacity for impact and also scalability. The capacity, or capability, of someone's impact is represented vertically, where their scalability, or the breadth of impact (local, national, or global), is then represented horizontally.

We tend to place value on other people's lives. Sports stars, musicians, and actors/actresses all carry a perceived value relative to their talent and skill (functional capacity). The beauty of scalability again is that it does not matter who someone is, how much money they make, where they live, or what they do for a living. We are all created equal in the eyes of the Lord, and all have equal opportunity to live in harmony with God thanks to the sacrifice of Jesus (Genesis 1:27; Acts 10:34; Romans 10:12; Galatians 3:28).

It is in God's economy that the degree of talent and skill are not a necessity to be influential. It is what is done with these resources that is the measuring stick for impact. For example, there could be a minor league baseball player with an incredible love for Jesus and is in the same way an ambassador for Christ who may never make the big leagues but will have a more profound impact in spreading the gospel than a hundred million-dollar big leaguer who has never spent any time or energy toward anyone outside his immediate circle of influence.

As Christians, service is a part of our nature and a spiritual discipline that helps exhibit our faith in action, which means service in and of itself is of no-compromise, but the scalability of that service is relative to our soul purpose.

We serve because Jesus as our model and the one we are

attempting to emulate served; therefore, it is detrimental to our faith in action for us to abandon a servant heart, essentially our soul purpose, toward others in Jesus's name.

Motivation for service to the Christian is a gauge for spiritual maturity and impact. We can serve others based on an innate desire deep down in our soul, or we can serve others at our convenience and because it makes us feel good.

A spiritually mature Christian will serve regardless of the day or hour of the need. Need will always trump convenience or pleasure, and there is little more detrimental to our faith than the inability to manage our time when convenience or pleasure is an obstacle. Jesus, in his most desperate hour, served his disciples without hesitation, showing that time was of the essence. (See the upper room discourse in John 13.)

Time may be one of the hardest resources that we personally get to manage. I have often failed to think of time as being a valuable commodity that needs to be managed wisely for God. But in reviewing the concept of margin, we see that time influences our ability to focus and give value to either things that are honoring to God or pleasing to us. And just like with time, free will, and our ability to align them with things that honor God, it is easy to venture off course.

Another example of how God's economy works can be seen in the military through the rank and promotion system. Sadly, rank ends up being something that an individual uses more for personal gain and less for blessing others. But for a Christ follower in the military, rank simply provides greater opportunity to serve and influence through servant leadership.

The concept of servant leadership is gaining traction both in the military and the private sector, but the concept genuinely aligns with our dialogue in this book in that it is about forgoing personal needs and desires of subordinates and focusing on the needs and desires of those who are being led, all the while having eyes fixed on Jesus. It is about not being concerned with getting recognition for a job well done, but instead praising those who helped make the mission a success.

While impact is evidence of faith in action, servant leadership is the relational connection that a leader has with those they are leading. It is the full character traits display of trustworthiness, transparency, integrity, humility, selfless service, and love (just to name a few) that separates servant leaders from those who have simply been given the responsibility to lead (Mark 10:42–45).

Just like Jesus did in his ministry, the servant leader puts the thoughts and needs of the group ahead of their own for the sake of leveraging the best talent, skills, and abilities from the group and making use of them for the betterment of the team and mission.

For a leader to live in impact according to the definition, a servant leader exhibits an innate focus on others in order to fulfill duties, responsibilities, and the mission while never taking their eyes off their soul purpose of giving honor and glory to God, even in a public square.

It is impossible for someone to live in impact in a servant leader capacity, while at the same time neglecting their soul purpose. If the duties, responsibilities, or mission do not align with God being able to receive glory for the work being done, it is encouraged that the individual compromise on their work and pursue other opportunities.

In 2019, after my deployment, I had it on my heart to work with a Christian band and bring them to our hometown for some Christian music and worship, something we don't often get to enjoy in our hometown. We had the resources and recognized that God was in the midst of the opportunity. Unbeknownst to us, in our community, planning was taking place to have a weekend-long Christian revival and music festival the month prior, as well as a Christian rock band at a separate event as part of a community ministry outreach to youth in our area.

Immediately upon finding out about not one, but two, rare

events and having a contract to bring Sanctus Real to Helena, I was frustrated. I was frustrated because what I was deeming as our personal resources and ticket sales for a concert that we had a two thousand-seat venue for now had significant competition in a town that doesn't do well with competition. My flesh was giving in to the desire to sell tickets instead of providing blessings.

In the midst of leading up to the event and realizing that attendance wasn't going to end up what we were anticipating when the agreement was made, it became apparent to me that my motivation was skewed and that this opportunity was not about quantity being ministered to, but instead about quality and opportunity. Recognizing the ticket sales were low gave us the ability to open the door to be a blessing to our local Christian K-12 school families by giving away tickets to families and teachers who may not have had the opportunity to go to the concert.

This experience taught me incredible lessons when it comes to managing God's resources. It taught me that no matter what I am preparing to embark upon, my heart has to be purely set on God's economic system, and if it is not, I have to be prepared for disappointment.

It also solidified the concept of *Chasing Impact* in that everything, when said and done about the experience, exuded my pursuit of offering spiritual value or enhancing others' lives through the desire to give God glory. It was difficult yet rewarding at the same time.

The whole reason we were able to bring Sanctus Real to our community was because of the financial blessing of deploying to Afghanistan as a chaplain, a journey made only possible by God's faithfulness to my call. And we desired to not keep this blessing for ourselves but instead share in this blessing with others.

The biggest blessings of that day in October 2019 were being able to meet and enjoy lunch with the guys in the band and see students' faces at our local Christian school light up as Dustin, Chris, and Mark came into their sanctuary as guests to share their musical talents and testimonies with them. No dollar amount can be placed on that experience, just as no dollar amount can be placed on impact.

> *Gold Nugget: The financial cost of an experience will never outweigh the spiritual blessings that come out of an experience when the pursuit is fulfilling one's soul purpose by giving glory to God.*

At the end of the day, Jesus was glorified, which is exactly what I realized after the fact was the genuine objective. I just had to come to understand that through perceiving the situation through the lens of faith.

When it comes to impact, the most important aspect to consider is the impact that is closest to you. Once Jesus had a group of men that he was mentoring and discipling, he never abandoned them. It was the apostles that he was adamantly focused on and never neglected. And while God may be calling you to global ministry or perhaps greater responsibilities in a secular environment, my personal encouragement is to always assess the impact you are making with those closest to you.

If we are failing at loving others, serving, or building connections with those closest to us because of pursuits outside this immediate purview or sphere of influence, we need to reevaluate our mission set in our hearts.

In light of WWJD (or "What Would Jesus Do"), I don't believe Jesus would be content with us if our actions and pursuits show that our priorities are far beyond those closest to us. God's resources will determine when and where opportunities arise, but it will never include abandoning responsibilities in relationships that God has ordained.

CHAPTER 9

THE BEGINNING OF SOMETHING EXTRAORDINARY

> For I was hungry and you gave me food, I was thirsty and you
> gave me drink, I was a stranger and you welcomed me, I was
> naked and you clothed me, I was sick and you visited me, I was
> in prison and you came to me ... And the King will answer
> them, "Truly, I say to you, as you did it to one of the least of
> these my brothers, you did it to me."
>
> —Matthew 25:35–36, 40

AS I BEGAN THE JOURNEY of writing this book, frankly a
journey that I was not sure what was in store for me except for
the fact that there were some stories to be told and truth to be
shared, the goal was simply to finish writing the book. And a lot
has happened in our world since I started writing.

There used to be a strong tendency for me to start something
but then get bored or miss finding the value or purpose in it, so
I would find something else to do. Some call this ADHD, but I
think God just says it is part of who he made me to be, and he has
a purpose for this attribute. What I have found is that anything
with great value and soul purpose has a higher probability to get
completed because it is not for my personal gain.

This work has brought back some memories and aspects of my life that are not shining moments, but without learning from the failures, I would have kept on going, trying to fill the pleasure tank to make things feel better. The failures and the successes are not mine to bear or claim. They are Jesus Christ's. Without him, I am nothing. My capacity is shallow and scalability narrow.

I hope that as you have made your way through the book, you have realized how important, or vital, perspective is in this pursuit of impact. Metaphorically speaking, if we are having trouble seeing, our eyes are blurry, or our glasses are dirty, we need to change how we perceive the world. Simply put, we have to make a change in order to see better. Sometimes the change is quick, with simply grabbing a lens-cleaning cloth, but sometimes it takes a process to see better, perhaps even a complete overhaul of the eye with Lasik surgery.

This is no different than when our worldview, or our perspective, is off. It may take getting back into the Bible after a few days, weeks, or even months being away from it, or it may take dusting the Bible off, getting into a church, and fellowshipping with believers to help in the process of reconfiguring a biblical worldview or perspective.

> Gold Nugget: It is not possible to see through a biblical lens without being actively engaged with God's Word, living among believers, and being in church on a regular basis.

As convenient as it would be, this is not feasible. And there is nothing biblical indicating living for Christ is convenient. In fact, it's quite the contrary. Sometimes God has us on a journey that we just can't figure out what he is doing, why he is doing it, and where we are going.

This is the case for me going back all the way to being a runner-up in a job interview in 2008 that I thought I really wanted with the Montana Army National Guard. Go figure, but I would have been a specialty recruiter, helping recruit and process new chaplains into the organization. This is prior to getting the call to the military chaplaincy.

The interview went well, but I was in competition with another strong candidate. When it was all said and done, I was the runner-up. That seems to happen quite a bit in my life. This can be tough for a competitive guy, but sanctification and spiritual growth has completely dismissed this competitive nature in me.

A few days after I found out I was not selected for the position, I got a call from the executive officer for the command, and he indicated that because I had developed a personal website for a business venture, they had wanted me to come work for them developing the new recruiting and retention website and helping in the marketing office.

This might seem minor, but the seed planted in the interview resulted in me being hired to create the website, which was probably one of the most significant moments of my life and the beginning of something extraordinary. I had no idea what was going to pan out over the long term, but God did.

Ironically, when I showed up on my first day to check out my new digs and meet my supervisor (a guy whom I gave a tour of the gym I worked at when he first moved to Helena a year prior), I looked at the iMac I would be working on and was completely intimidated because I had never seen an iMac, let alone worked on one, and this was going to be the computer that was mine to design the site with. I had no idea how to even turn the machine on.

While working for Jon and with two other Christian men, Chad and Noah, as part of the leadership team, they invited me to join them in the mornings for a workout that they called Mighty Men, named after the men in King David's life who were responsible for his security, his entourage.

Again, there was more intimidation because in this morning routine we worked out, read, and memorized passages from the book of James. We prayed together, shared vulnerabilities in our lives, and held each other accountable as men of faith. This was legitimately the first time in my life that I had a desire to open up and study the Word of God with other men. There was a brotherhood in this group that I had never experienced before. These men were the first true examples in the military of Christian men who had strong day-to-day mentorship and influence in my life. And to this day, I consider them brothers in the faith.

Despite my shortcomings, despite me being an E-5, they showed grace, love, encouragement, and the character of Mighty Men that I needed in my life. These were a senior noncommissioned officer and a junior and senior officer who took me under their wing to mentor me, and they were tremendous blessings then and are still tremendous blessings to me now. Shortly after that, I realized God was tugging on my heart to follow him into the chaplaincy.

There is so much more that can be included in this part of the story that I will spare, but after working in the recruiting and retention command, I followed this up by finding a passion for supporting Montana National Guard Service members and their families in the Yellow Ribbon Reintegration Program. Again, this was after an experience of being selected for a position as the state sexual assault response coordinator and later finding out I was not eligible for the position due to a conflict of interest as a chaplain candidate.

Regardless of that determination, God had me on the right path, honing much-needed skills and perspective on how to care for and serve our Montana warriors and their families during the deployment cycle. So much of the impact I have been fortunate enough to be involved in has come about as a result of these five years in the Yellow Ribbon Program.

While in the Yellow Ribbon Program and working for another mentor, Brigadier General (Ret.) Jeffrey Ireland, I was able to recognize a strong need in Montana that would prove to be a much greater need than what the Yellow Ribbon Program had the ability to support.

In December 2014, I lost my job with the Yellow Ribbon Reintegration Program due to federal funding cuts, and the next week I was working on a plan that would establish Impact Montana.

I write all this to share that when we let go and let God take the reins, opportunity gets presented, and impact generated. It has not always been easy. I have thrown up my hands at times asking God, "Why me?" And now it all makes perfect sense.

I have had many conversations with peers about not being a pastor in a church as a chaplain, but again, that was not the path God put me on. This path, an ambassador for Christ, speaking truth in a world that needs it more now than ever, is not confined by ministry in a church. And just like me, you are called to live out your faith in this same manner.

So I will continue to follow God's lead and always be joyful coming in second place because second place is where I find God simply telling me that is not where he wants me to be, and he has something different in store for me.

As I prepare to finish up *Chasing Impact*, I am also closing the book on a personal chapter. I am closing the chapter on a career in the military after twenty-one years. It is a career that if I would have done it my way, it would have ended after my deployment in 2005 at six years. But there was always that little tug on my heart that said, "No, you are not done yet. There is still work to be done."

The old cliché of "when one door closes, another one opens" has certainly been the case as God has continued to open doors throughout this journey, even after praying for doors to close at times when things got hard. What I am genuinely excited about is seeing what is behind the next door and a part of the next book.

In the work we have done through Impact Montana, I have found tremendous blessings in being able to help individuals reconnect to purpose and reestablish identity outside the uniform and essentially become the best versions of themselves they can be through support relative to the veteran thrive factors. And more importantly, many of the veterans we serve are seeking and turning their lives over to Jesus and identifying their "whys".

We have seen some incredible transformations by helping individuals get connected to service providers that may not be part of the mainstream health model, yet the results have been anything but mainstream. And most importantly, we have helped individuals rediscover the best part of themselves by promoting holistic health and wellness through the veteran thrive factors.

As I personally move forward and glean what has been learned from the Impact Montana support realm, it is in my personal interest to share the impact model that expands the concept of impact and will be a broader support system that offers networking, mentorship, and the newly developed training for individuals from all walks of life, not just Montana service members, veterans, and their families.

IMPACT MODEL

The model has been derived from several years of engaging with soldiers who navigate typical life challenges (most of which can be addressed through a perspective shift), as well as with the training curricula that the military uses for personal, family, and professional development and being able to promote one's (or a family unit's) ability to thrive and pursue impact.

The uniqueness of the impact model is that it is not your typical skill development or behavior modification tool; instead it is dedicated to promoting and targeting specific areas that have the ability to pragmatically develop a plan that will slow someone down and reconnect to the most important things in life, the things that help them thrive.

There are five components to the impact model, with perspective/worldview being the primary component, or cornerstone, that is key to all the other components. If the perspective or worldview is not established or is fluid, the capacity of impact is drastically limited. Optimally, one has a specific worldview, or cornerstone, that they are operating from, and whatever it is will determine the potential outcomes and certainly the capacity for impact. If there is not an existing worldview, then this is a great conversation to have to support the importance of this foundation being laid.

Beyond perspective/worldview, the model suggests values, mindset, goals, and then performance, in this specific order, as being the additional four components that complete the impact model. The impact model and the auxiliary components to *Chasing Impact* are not intended to be complex; in fact, it's quite the opposite.

To review, the intention of *Chasing Impact* is to simply help individuals slow down, take a step back and consider priorities, where energy is gained and lost, and help prescribe a plan to thrive contextually through a faith-based lens and, when thriving, be able to chase the casted vision set forth.

The impact model and its complementary considerations can be found at www.chasingimpact.com.

If there is anything that I hope to articulate well in this book, it is that thriving is about us maximizing our capacity in order to be fruitful in influencing others. You are more than just a number or statistic, and because of this, the assessment is not for research purposes but instead for supporting individuals discovering their prescription for thriving. One may consider this a relational investment and opportunity for growth. We as Christians are called to be relational in our ministry.

The only other component of the thrive factor model that I want to address here at the end of the book is performance. We often get wrapped up in attempting to perform in order to gain accolades from our peers, those in authority over us at work, or other relationships we may be in that warrant accolades. But the truth of the matter is that this is typically for personal gain and not an indicator of where one's heart lies.

When one is intentional every day, engaged, and does not compromise in spiritual disciplines and their other thrive factors, personal accolades are irrelevant. Our pursuit for accolades should be of the spiritual reward variety, not secular.

Naturally, if you work in a secular environment and you are thriving, you will receive accolades. I am not saying that you should not care how others evaluate your performance. The evaluation from others should be motivating instead of debilitating, a motivator to "fight the good fight of the faith" (1 Timothy 6:11). And regardless of the performance evaluation, the model is intended to provide value to output relative to the components of the model.

Impact may not look the way you intended, just like what I have experienced looks nothing like what I imagined my life to be at this point, but that is testament to letting go and letting God be in the driver's seat. Impact is a by-product of faith. And even though it may not look the way you intended, it will result in the way it is supposed to be, all for God's purpose and, at the end of the day, glory.

Even though I can't define what impact looks like for you, I can caution you that it will likely be uncomfortable at times, testing your faith and endurance, and as I have attempted to share, it will result in the laying down of your life in some way, shape, or form, which is up to and including death (Philippians 1:21). Are you committed to that kind of impact?

CONCLUSION

STARTING SMALL

In my work with individuals who are struggling, more often than not, the struggle is so significant that even having a place to start can be difficult. In this case, impact is not even a consideration. Starting small is paramount in the journey toward thriving.

I have seen it. Men and women who have no hope, feel like they are drowning, or are like the rocks that we discussed previously have to start simply. It starts with prayer and reading a chapter in one of the gospels or visiting a church on Sunday and hearing a message of hope. It starts by taking a one-mile walk. It starts by going out to dinner with your significant other or spending an hour with one of your children. Or maybe it is cutting up a credit card that has you in a financial hole so deep that you don't feel like you can get out of it. It may even start with immediate meditation and prayer for recentering. It doesn't matter where, just that the important first step, a small step, is taken to start and trust that God is with you and will never forsake you.

The spiritual refuge and hope that we seek in this chaotic life are only found through Jesus Christ. It cannot be found through prescription medications that promise to take away pain or stress. Refuge cannot be found through financial prosperity or a career that makes us feel good. And government or politicians certainly are not able to give us refuge. These things do not save us from our sin; they do not offer identity or purpose and unequivocally cannot give us a complete understanding of love. Only Jesus does.

If this book has offered encouragement or motivation to make changes in your life, come join in the pursuit of making a difference and share your story of how this book has positively influenced you at www.chasingimpact.com. At our website you will find more resources and support to assist in your journey of chasing impact.

9 781664 231900